'Jo's insights, stories and drawing
between God, people and the res
together to demonstrate why lool
part of the Christian life.'
Dr Ruth Bancewicz, church engagement .... institute for
Science and Religion

'Jo Swinney's delightful, engaging and provocative Lenten devotional is aptly named. So often we tell a truncated Easter story, but this series of reflections opens us out to the depth, breadth and grandeur of God's love for his whole creation, including us people. Narrated with honesty, warmth and the insightful perspective of a storyteller, *The Whole Easter Story* helps us see afresh the immense power and wisdom of the cross for the salvation of the whole world. Thoroughly recommended!'
Professor Paul S. Williams, chief executive, Bible Society

'Do something different this Lent! This is your chance to look at the relationships between God, people and the environment in an entirely new way. Join Jo Swinney of A Rocha as she takes us on a special journey through Lent, accompanied by birds, bugs, mammals, reptiles and, yes, people!'
Martin Hodson, principal tutor of Christian Rural and Environmental Studies

'Digging into scripture from the starting point of God's ongoing work of creation and not human sin – this is the Lenten journey the church needs to take for the sake of the world. Honest, accessible, deeply informed by practices of both faith and conservation, this is a book that really could reshape how contemporary Christians see the world and find their place in it.'
Dr Ellen Davis, professor of Bible and Practical Theology, Duke Divinity School

'*The Whole Easter Story* is both intensely personal and mind-bendingly cosmic, as well as being a really good read!'
The Revd Dr Dave Bookless, head of theology, A Rocha International

'*The Whole Easter Story* is a series of thoughtful reflections on the story of God's salvation through Israel and, ultimately, in Christ. Yet, at the same time, Jo Swinney delightfully weaves in her musings on the familiar rhythms of our ordinary lives and her pondering on the beauty which we all behold in creation. I warmly commend these Easter reflections to all!'
Dr Lai Pak-Wah, principal, Biblical Graduate School of Theology, Singapore

'It is easy to feel small or powerless in tackling big questions of the environment. That is why this companion to Lent is essential reading for churches: it guides us in thinking through these problems, not only as individuals, but ultimately as communities that care and as people who have a joined-up way of telling the whole Easter story with a heart for the creation God loves. Beautifully timed, this book needs to be read, listened to, discussed, prayed with, carried in a pocket and acted on.'
The Revd Dr Ivan Khovacs, Canterbury Christ Church University and St James's Church Piccadilly

'This is a truly enjoyable devotional book, providing an excellent guide as we journey through our relationship with God, others and God's wider creation, as well as God's own relationship with his creation. It draws deeply from scripture, with insights that will have you wanting to re-read familiar Bible stories. Refreshingly honest, laugh out loud, attentive to all of God's creation – your heart and soul will be fed.'
Jo Herbert-James, head of engagement, A Rocha UK

JO SWINNEY

The WHOLE Easter Story

WHY THE CROSS IS GOOD NEWS FOR ALL CREATION

BRF Ministries

 Ministries

15 The Chambers, Vineyard
Abingdon OX14 3FE
+44 (0)1865 319700 | brf.org.uk

Bible Reading Fellowship (BRF) is a charity (233280)
and company limited by guarantee (301324),
registered in England and Wales

ISBN 978 1 80039 269 4
First published 2024
10 9 8 7 6 5 4 3 2 1 0
All rights reserved

Text © Jo Swinney 2024
This edition © Bible Reading Fellowship 2024
Cover illustration © Jo Swinney; design © Dan Nolloth

The authors assert the moral right to be identified as the authors of this work

Acknowledgements

Unless otherwise stated, scripture quotations are taken from The Holy Bible, New International Version (Anglicised edition) copyright © 1979, 1984, 2011 by Biblica. Used by permission of Hodder & Stoughton Publishers, an Hachette UK company. All rights reserved. 'NIV' is a registered trademark of Biblica. UK trademark number 1448790.

Scripture quotation marked 'NLT' are taken from The Holy Bible, New Living Translation, copyright © 1996, 2004, 2007, 2013. Used by permission of Tyndale House Publishers, Inc., Carol Stream, Illinois 60188. All rights reserved.

Every effort has been made to trace and contact copyright owners for material used in this resource. We apologise for any inadvertent omissions or errors, and would ask those concerned to contact us so that full acknowledgement can be made in the future.

A catalogue record for this book is available from the British Library

Printed and bound by CPI Group (UK) Ltd, Croydon CR0 4YY

Dedicated to
Grace Sogbey, Alex Simiyu and Shanitah Nalukenge
and the rest of the A Rocha Comms Collective –
creative and courageous tellers of the whole story.

Photocopying for churches

Please report to CLA Church Licence any photocopy you make from this publication. Your church administrator or secretary will know who manages your CLA Church Licence.

The information you need to provide to your CLA Church Licence administrator is as follows:

Title, Author, Publisher and ISBN

If your church doesn't hold a CLA Church Licence, information about obtaining one can be found at **uk.ccli.com**

Contents

List of illustrations 9

Introduction 11

I God and people

1 Created 21
2 Loved 25
3 Judged 29
4 In covenant 33
5 Understood 37
6 Being saved 41
7 Forgiven 45
8 Reconciled 49
9 Renewed 53
10 Made eternal 57

II God and creation

11 Whose world is it? 63
12 Under his command 67
13 Glimpses of glory 71
14 Sabbath for the land 75
15 Impacted by the fall 79
16 God's covenant with all life 83
17 Jesus and creation 87
18 Promised redemption 90
19 Earthly hope 94
20 Heaven is coming here 98

III People and people

21 A brotherhood of man 103
22 Forgive, forgive, forgive, repeat 107
23 Costly love 111
24 Banking on each other 115
25 One for all and all for one 119
26 The mind of Christ 123
27 Unity and diversity 127
28 Obedient love 131
29 Running the race 134
30 Mercy mixed with fear 138

IV People and creation

31 The first mission 145
32 Wicked living 149
33 Consequences 153
34 All creatures of our God 157
35 Learning from the lilies 161
36 Eyes to see 164
37 Small mercies 168
38 Back in our place 171
39 Children, wolves and cobras 175
40 Joined in worship 179

Six-week group discussion guide 183

Notes 187

List of illustrations

Alongside each of the 40 reflections I have drawn an illustration of a species supported by A Rocha's work around the world. I hope that these amateur sketches might lead to increased wonder at our creator God's magnificent ingenuity and care in bringing the cosmos into being.

1   Salish sucker 24
2   Sokoke scops owl 28
3   European roller 32
4   Horseshoe crab 36
5   Indian elephant 40
6   White-naped mangabey 44
7   Halavi guitarfish 48
8   European storm petrel 52
9   Oregon forestsnail 56
10 Tiger 60
11 Tree frog 66
12 Huarango/algarrobo 70
13 Red-tailed hawk 74
14 Long-tailed bat 78
15 Grey-headed flying fox 82
16 Yellow-banded bumblebee 86
17 Barn owl 89
18 Northern red-legged frog 93
19 Grey-faced petrel/ōi 97
20 European hedgehog 100

21	Norfolk hawker	106
22	Ocellated lizard	110
23	Atewa slippery frog	114
24	Southern festoon	118
25	Hermit butterfly	122
26	Crisp pillow coral	126
27	Camphor thyme	130
28	European pond terrapin	133
29	Kentish plover	137
30	Clarke's weaver	141
31	Garry oak	148
32	White-throated dipper	152
33	Geometric tortoise	156
34	Kelp	160
35	Black-headed lapwing	163
36	Weaver's fritillary	167
37	Keeled skimmer	170
38	Russell's viper	174
39	Three-toothed orchid	178
40	Honey badger	182

Introduction

Lent arrives just as we are forced to acknowledge that our New Year's resolutions have been, yet again, empty aspirations. And while we know it is, in principle, A Very Good Thing, Lent can bear with it the same whiff of failure. These six weeks offer us an annual opportunity to reflect and prepare for Easter Sunday, so that when the day arrives, we are primed to experience the impact of the resurrection once again. But like me, you might find most years you start strong on Shrove Tuesday with a pancake or five, then give up chocolate and/or wine for a few days, but soon drift back into the usual patterns before Holy Week sneaks up on you, and you realise you've wasted another Lent.

Perhaps part of the reason we are so disengaged is a sense of overfamiliarity with the story. The tension, the intrigue and the key players are too well known to us. We can see around every corner; we could recite the dialogue. I'm so glad you have chosen *The Whole Easter Story* to be your companion this year, and I hope together we will discover a new and more expansive outlook on the trial, death and resurrection of Christ.

Often when considering the Easter story, we think in terms of what it means for our personal relationship with God. We are children of our times and places and – in wealthier societies anyway – we have a current obsession with the self. We are all about our own individual growth, purpose and spirituality. There is no doubt that each of us has our own space in our maker's heart and indeed a place in the Easter story, but what happened on the cross is not just a story of me and Jesus. It is far deeper and wider than that.

Over the 40 days of Lent, we'll be exploring what Easter means for God's relationship not only with us but also with the whole of creation, and how that changes our relationships with each other and our relationship with creation. The death and resurrection of Jesus changes everything.

There are four sections of ten days each, to be read from Mondays to Saturdays between Ash Wednesday and Easter Day. On Sundays we'll rest!

About A Rocha

Throughout this book you will find reference to an organisation called A Rocha, so some context might be useful before we start. To declare my personal stake, my parents were among the founders, and I am now the director of communications for A Rocha International.

A Rocha means 'The Rock' in Portuguese. It began as a field study centre and bird observatory in the Algarve in 1983 from a conviction that, as the 'earth is the Lord's, and everything in it' (Psalm 24:1), worship of the Lord must include caring well for what is his. The late theologian John Stott, a great friend to A Rocha, wrote the following in the foreword to *Under the Bright Wings*, which tells the story of the early days:

> Christian people should surely have been in the vanguard of the movement for environmental responsibility, because of our doctrines of creation and stewardship. Did God make the world? Does he sustain it? Has he committed its resources to our care? His personal concern for his own creation should be sufficient to inspire us to be equally concerned.[1]

A Rocha is now present in six continents. We are the only global Christian nature conservation charity, although increasing numbers of Christians are engaging in creation care, as evidenced by the more than 7,000 churches that have signed up to A Rocha UK's Eco Church programme. In Kenya, a boardwalk through the mangroves funds local children's secondary school education, so their families no longer need to fell the trees of Arabuko Sokoke Forest to pay for it. In Lebanon, an area of wasteland where burnt-out tanks once rotted has been restored and is now a public park. In Canada, deprived and disadvantaged communities are supplied with nourishing organic produce from our farm. In Ghana, we have taken the government to court for their intention to allow Atewa Forest to be levelled for bauxite extraction, breaching human rights for clean water and the right of species to existence. In India, we work to make peace between the elephant and human communities around Bannerghatta National Park. In all this, and the very many other ways we protect and care for the places in which we're rooted, we endeavour to do what my father in his book calls 'writing the gospel in the landscape'.

Mary Magdalene's story

As we consider the Easter story in the days and weeks to come, we will be dipping in and out of a wide range of biblical texts. It would be good to look at the core narrative before we set out, which can be found in all four gospels (Matthew 26—28; Mark 15—16; Luke 22—24; John 19—20), and I highly recommend you find the time to revisit all these accounts. What follows is my attempt to see the crucifixion and resurrection of Jesus through the eyes of someone Matthew, Mark, Luke and John all record as having been close to these events – Mary Magdalene. We have been given enough colour and detail to have a good sense of what she experienced, although my imagination and a bit of extratextual research has helped to fill out some of what follows.

We have rested through two more sabbaths since Jesus left us for the second time. The first time we believed him dead. We won't make that mistake again. So we are not in grief, though we often talk about what it was like to have him right there, passing the bread, throwing back his head in laughter, messing with the children's hair. It felt so normal at the time, and now we can see how very far from ordinary those short years with him really were. And the last months, travelling in Galilee – I will be feasting on the memories all the days I have left. He has given his Spirit, but I miss having his body around.

Joanna and I were talking again this morning about what happened at Passover. At first it was hard to find any words for the images, the sounds and smells, the paralysing horror of what they did to him. Never mind that he came through it with only a few scars, we saw what we saw. We had to live through two whole days before the miracle of the third made it right. Now our tongues have loosened, and the words flow like the Jordan after the rains. As you are here, you can be my audience. Be warned, though, it is not easy to tell, and it won't be easy to hear either.

I'll start from when I saw the crowd turn nasty. You could say I should have seen it coming, given Jesus had been saying loud and clear exactly what was going to happen, but I was utterly in denial. I thought justice would prevail and he'd be released. He had done nothing wrong after all. But there was a moment when people all around me started shouting the same thing, one united voice: 'Crucify him! Crucify him!' The wave of sound almost visibly hit Pilate mid-sentence, and in the pit of my stomach I knew: they were going to have their way. I'm sure many there were among those waving palm branches and treating him like royalty only days ago, even among those he'd touched with his kind, healing hands, or those who had trailed behind him as he travelled and taught, hanging on his every word. Now they were a pack of baying dogs scenting raw meat. My skin prickled with fear.

The next time I saw him he was in a crush of soldiers in the Praetorium. They had stripped off his robe and replaced it with a garish purple costume meant to make a mockery of the idea he was any kind of king. His mother and I were close enough to see that his undergarment was soggy with blood. He was barely able to stand.

Introduction 15

I've heard how brutal a Roman flogging can be, flaying through skin into muscle and even chipping bone. Lord, have mercy.

To the robe they added a crown. Not one of gold with the finest rubies and precious stones the world has to offer. Even that would have been woefully inadequate. But these brutes found it amusing to crown him with woven thorns. He could have called down battalions of avenging angels; he could have struck them blind with one moment of unveiled glory. Instead, they slapped his face and spat and tried to outdo each other's stupid insults. How could we watch? I honestly don't know. But it felt important to be with him, to witness.

Eventually the hilarity came to an end, and it was down to business. They redressed him in his own cloak, a cloak I had washed myself many times. I knew its texture; I had scrubbed it and handed it back to him clean, smelling as fresh as the Galilean air. How to explain what it was like to see those soldiers throw it over his battered shoulders? Or to stand by helpless as he staggered under the weight of the enormous wooden crossbeam?

In the early morning light, we were on the move, a throng pressing through the wakening city streets and beyond the walls to Golgotha. Jesus was too broken and exhausted to make any progress, so they pulled in a passer-by and transferred the cross to him. Although there were still those who were clearly enjoying every moment, the main sound was the women's weeping. John heard Jesus tell some of them not to cry for him but to save their tears for themselves, especially if they had children. What did he know? I've been trying not to wonder too much about that.

You can't live in the Roman Empire without knowing what a crucifixion involves. I've seen crosses in the distance. I knew it to be one of the most humiliating and painful ways a person could be killed. We came out on to the open hillside, and the crowd spread out. I noticed birdsong and a cluster of delicate white flowers at my feet. I saw my toe was cut and bleeding and thought it might as well be someone else's foot for all I could feel it.

Three people were to be executed. Jesus was the first. The soldiers pulled every last piece of clothing off him, and pushed him down on to his back, stretching his arms along the crossbar. In the stillness, each strike of the mallet pushing iron into wood through flesh resounded, clear as a bell. One wrist, then the next. Salome retched and stumbled away to empty her stomach in the undergrowth. Mary and I were like one piece of stone, leaning together, fixed in place.

The three men now nailed in place were raised up on their awaiting shafts, Jesus in the middle. There was a sign on his cross, 'King of the Jews' written out three times, in Aramaic, Latin and Greek to make sure everyone caught the joke. The guards were full of bravado. 'Why aren't you saving yourself? Think you're so powerful, then prove it!' And Jesus? He was so dignified, so fully himself, even then, even in more pain than I can imagine. He asked God to forgive them, while they drew lots for his stuff.

Those of us women who had been with Jesus for the last few months, caring for him, following him through the villages and towns of Galilee, I'm proud to say we stayed close for those gruesome six hours when he hung on the edge of life. He could see us from up there. And we watched as he fought for each agonising gulp of air, while he cried out in the desolation of his Father's absence.

And then things became very strange. As the sun hit its highest point it disappeared, and an eerie darkness fell. The spring warmth was gone in an instant. For three hours we huddled together in the gloom. At three o clock, pandemonium: the voice of Jesus echoed over the hill, 'It is finished,' and then he was dead. The ground shook violently, and the same soldiers so full of themselves all day were sobbing and shaking in fright. One of them seemed to be experiencing some kind of religious ecstasy. Later we heard the temple curtain had ripped top to bottom, and dead people had burst out of tombs, full of life.

The shock of his death still wakes me like a lightning bolt from deepest sleep. I sit up, my heart racing, my cheeks damp with tears. Mary, I tell myself, this was not the end of the story. All is well.

We continued to sit by the cross for some time, unsure what would happen and unwilling to leave his body just hanging there. The other two men stayed alive until almost sundown, and if it hadn't been for the sabbath who knows how long they would have taken to die. Once their legs had been broken, it was a matter of horrible minutes. I suppose to make sure he really had gone, a soldier plunged his spear into Jesus' side, and a gush of watery blood poured on to the ground.

Kind men we later knew as Nicodemus and Joseph took charge of the body. Mary and I followed them to a garden close by, and watched as they wrapped it in linen strips with myrrh and aloes. There was a newly made tomb dug into the rock. Once the body was inside, they managed to roll an enormous stone over the mouth. A Roman guard sealed it, before pushing his shoulders back and standing to attention.

We eventually went back together to my home, where we passed the next day quietly, in observance of the sabbath. If you have lost someone you love, you will know how our sorrow crushed us, how our tears wracked us and brought no relief, how we could barely think for the noisy questions racing around our minds.

Neither of us slept that night, and it was still dark when we gathered burial spices and set off for the tomb. The air was cool and the ground damp with dew. Mary kept circling around the problem of how the two of us would manage to get in, given the size of the stone blocking the way. As it turns out, that wasn't an issue.

I was the first to see the stone was missing and my immediate thought was that dear Jesus' body had been stolen. I couldn't bear it – a desecration too many. I ran ahead, and bending down could see there was no body in there, only the cloth. I might have lost it, but in that instant the most intense, clean light filled the space and an angel in white spoke to me. The angel said, 'Why are you looking for the living among the dead? Jesus has risen, just as he told you he would!' All of a sudden I remembered. He had told us he would die. And he had told us he would come back from the dead.

This is the part of the story I love most. I will never tire of telling it. I will never stop reliving it. The living, resurrected Jesus was there in the garden, and he said my name. I was so overwhelmed I crumpled to the ground, my face literally in the mud at his feet, laughing and crying at the same time. I was clutching his robe in my fists, and he was gently trying to disentangle himself. He said, so full of affection and love, 'Don't hold on to me! You need to go and tell the others that I'm back.' I would have done anything for him, so I let go, got to my feet and left to share the news.

Of course they didn't believe me, but that's what it's like being a woman. And they got to see him for themselves eventually. How about you? Do you believe me?

God and people

LET ME BEGIN by telling you two short stories. Federica was for much of her life, by her own account, a cynical atheist who rarely gave the concept of God a thought. A journalist who had covered everything from human trafficking to the plight of Syrian refugees in Lebanon, to the epicentre of the Covid pandemic in her hometown in Italy, a relationship breakdown and the isolation of lockdown took her to a dark place. Having a sense that being immersed in nature might bring healing, she jumped on a flight to Kenya, and stumbled on the A Rocha field study centre at the coast. Seeing reference to Christianity on the website, Federica pictured nuns coming between her and the sunset beer she hoped to enjoy on the beach, and she was almost deterred from completing her booking. But she was intrigued by the conservation going on and ended up pushing ahead.

She planned to stay for a couple of days. In the end she was there for several weeks, returning a year later to be baptised in the Indian Ocean. From seeing the tender round-the-clock care the A Rocha team gave to an injured bird, to joining times of worship and finding intellectual hurdles could be leapt with mental integrity intact, Federica's mind and heart were won over and she gave her life to Jesus.[2]

My younger daughter, Charis, showed fierce animosity towards God from when she was a tiny child. Once she had mastered the word 'No', she applied it to invitations to pray at bedtime, to read Bible stories or to go to church. Her older sister, Alexa, would earnestly try to bring her into the fold. On one memorable occasion, I overheard Charis shouting 'Jesus is a sausage' at the top of her lungs. It was all rather baffling – I haven't ever come across another case of such a young person opposing their parents' faith as strongly.

When she was six, we were at a big Christian camp and she came back from a children's session with a bit of paper that said, 'Charis gave her life to Jesus this morning.' We wondered if they had got the wrong end of the stick; perhaps she had stood up to go to the toilet and been included in an altar call head count? But Charis had indeed become a Christian. She had been all out. She was now all in. As a teenager she continues to challenge and inspire me in my own faith journey and she's one of the most Spirit-filled evangelists I know.

People are made for relationship with God. And yet since our earliest days as a species, we have communally and individually had the tendency to damage and even sever that relationship. In any given train carriage, football stadium or shopping mall around the world, those who would say they knew God personally would be in a small minority.

In these first ten days of Lent, we'll be thinking about God and us: what was the intention at creation; what went wrong and continues to go wrong; how does Jesus' crucifixion allow us to reconcile?

Day 1

Created

For you created my inmost being;
    you knit me together in my mother's womb.
I praise you because I am fearfully and wonderfully made;
    your works are wonderful,
    I know that full well.
My frame was not hidden from you
    when I was made in the secret place,
    when I was woven together in the depths of the earth.
Your eyes saw my unformed body;
    all the days ordained for me were written in your book
    before one of them came to be.
PSALM 139:13–16

I have twice had the strange experience of growing a human in my body. At first the only evidence of their existence was a pink line on a plastic stick. After a few weeks they made me feel very sick, and then they grew big enough to give me a bump and a great deal of discomfort. When I look at my teenage daughters, I find it hard to connect these beautiful, fully grown and increasingly independent people with anything that might have gone on inside me. We may have sophisticated scanning equipment now that makes the womb slightly less secret, but I can still relate to the idea that babies develop in 'the depths of the earth', a process shrouded in mystery and deep darkness.

I can also confirm that I was not a consciously active participant in the task of taking Alexa and Charis from being a couple of cells to fully formed babies. It was God who created them, who breathed life into their beings, who gave them their fingerprints, their temperaments, their quirks and tendencies. As humans we have become very clever in certain regards. We know our bodies are composed of oxygen, hydrogen, nitrogen, carbon, calcium, phosphorus, sulphur, potassium, sodium, chlorine and magnesium, among other elements. But we have no clue how to combine those elements into a living, breathing, emotional and spiritual being.

As we begin to consider our relationship with God in the context of the Easter story, a good place to start is with the fact he is creator, and we are created. We were created as *Homo sapiens*, a distinct species among many, imprinted with the very image of God (Genesis 1:27), and we were each and every one of us created, seen, significant and loved before one of our days came to be.

I have heard the story told from a different starting point, as I imagine you have. Sometimes it is told like this: people are awful; we are dirty, sinful, horrid things, and we took God right to the end of his tether, so he had to come and die for us.

I found a website giving step-by-step instructions for evangelism, and this is step two (step one was about sin too):

> Write the word 'SIN' vertically between the words 'MAN' and 'GOD'. Quote Romans 3:23 – 'For all have sinned and fall short of the glory of God.' Questions to ask: 'What does the word "all" in this verse mean? Does it include you?' Always use questions after giving a verse so that you may know whether its truth is getting across. Say, 'Since God is holy and man is sinful, sin separates man from God.'[3]

But the Bible doesn't start with sin; it starts with creation, and that makes all the difference to how we understand our relationship with God. Let's dig into Psalm 139 and you'll see what I mean.

Psalms are songs reflecting the experience of their authors' lives with God and infused with references to early sections of scripture, books of history, prophecy, poetry and apocalypse. They were written long before the life of Jesus, but in the understanding that all too often humankind was failing, corporately and individually, to keep their side of the covenant promises that framed their relationship with God. King David led his people into so many bloody battles that he was forbidden from building a temple. His relationship history would definitely have earned him a well-deserved 'Love Rat' tabloid splash. He worshipped God with all his heart but sometimes cursed him too. In all this complexity, one thing was clear: as a being created by God, he knew his intrinsic worth was never up for debate – 'Your works are wonderful' (v. 14).

David's language in Psalm 139 describes a very hands-on process of making – he uses words like 'knit' and 'woven'. These crafts involve patterns, but patterns which allow for creativity. Each human is like others, and at the same time unique. We are wired with a need for significance, to have a place, to be seen and known as an individual, not just a speck in a blurry crowd of billions, and thankfully we have a God with the capacity to relate to each of us – 'Your eyes saw [me]… all the days ordained for me were written in your book' (v. 16). We can base our self-esteem on everything from an annual appraisal at work, to the number of hearts under our Instagram posts, to how many people show up to our birthday drinks, but why would we? Each of us has been 'fearfully and wonderfully made' (v. 14) by our ever-loving creator God.

For reflection

Think about some of the people who have shaped how you see yourself, from parents to teachers, to friends and spouses, to employers and media figures. How much power have you given their voices? How can you let God's voice speak more loudly, and what would change if you decided to listen only to him when it comes to your worth?

Prayer

Abba, Father, I am yours. You meant me to be here, and you look at me with love and pleasure. Your knowledge of me is deeper than I can fathom. My feelings, motivations and impulses are laid bare before you. I can't deceive you; I can't hide from you. Thank you that your commitment to me is unshakeable. Amen.

Salish sucker *Catostomus sp. cf. catostomus*

A small freshwater fish thought to be locally extinct – until it was identified in the Little Campbell River watershed (British Columbia, Canada) in 2011! The population is now thriving.

Day 2

Loved

> I pray that out of his glorious riches he may strengthen you with power through his Spirit in your inner being, so that Christ may dwell in your hearts through faith. And I pray that you, being rooted and established in love, may have power, together with all the Lord's holy people, to grasp how wide and long and high and deep is the love of Christ, and to know this love that surpasses knowledge – that you may be filled to the measure of all the fullness of God.
> EPHESIANS 3:16–19

'Jesus loves you.' Was there ever a sentiment rendered so toothless by its application to fridge magnets, bumper stickers and billboards? But it isn't just kitschy design or overuse that makes it a difficult idea to properly absorb. There are good reasons for this prayer of Paul's for the Ephesian church, which are worth our while exploring. One of them is that we need God's help to grasp the dimensions of Christ's love.

Why do we find it hard? I can think of a few reasons, and I'm sure you could add to them. First, we use ourselves as a reference point and our kind of love is human, not divine. Even at its best, our love is enmeshed in self-interest. It is often confused with lust, dependence, and a desire for power or possession. This definition submitted to the Urban Dictionary by a user known as 'The Kinkionary' hints at how muddled it can get:

> Love is a dangerous investment, but if it works, it will be the best investment you will ever make. People pay for love, people kill for love, and love can do crazy things to a mind. If you are in

love you know it. I am in love and it is the greatest feeling in the world, you are in a good mood all the time.[4]

How hard it is then to understand a love that – let's face it – surpasses knowledge, that takes the best of what we are able to give to and have ever received from a fellow *Homo sapiens* and blows it out of the water.

Secondly, it is far easier to understand love when it comes from someone we can see, touch, feel and hear. Yet the greatest love we could ever know is of someone who dwells 'in our hearts through faith' (see v. 17). It is a matter of our 'inner being'. In this life, we won't feel the literal arms of Jesus around us, see the expression on his face when he looks at us, or hear his audible voice tell us how completely and dependably he loves us. That will come one day, and there is a myriad of ways he does speak love to us, but it is all more mysterious and intangible than I'd like it to be, if I'm honest.

Thirdly, we are more comfortable receiving love from someone when we understand why they love us and we can reciprocate in kind. I have a friend whose husband forgave her for an affair. Years later she still experiences acute discomfort in the acceptance of love she feels she doesn't deserve. Part of her even wishes he would have an affair so that she could offer him an equivalent gift of grace to even things out. Jesus poured out his life for those who were either indifferent or openly hateful towards him: 'God demonstrates his own love for us in this: while we were still sinners, Christ died for us' (Romans 5:8).

We can probably all agree it isn't easy to grasp Christ's love, but it is in this love we are able to live. As Jesus often did, Paul uses agricultural language here. A plant sends out roots into the soil that can provide water, nutrients and stability, but it must then get established – settled in its place so that it can survive and grow. We should be 'rooted and established in love' (v. 17). And not just any love, but the love of God.

Here is something to catch and reflect on. The death of Jesus did not make God able to love us. It was an expression of a love that already existed. Perhaps you didn't need to have that spelt out, but I have heard enough people refer to the 'God of the Old Testament' as though this is a different, harsher and more vengeful version, that I think it bears saying. From before creation to after new creation, God is love. In and between and through the Trinity is love.

One of the disciples referred to himself as 'the disciple Jesus loved' throughout his written account of Jesus' life, the gospel of John. My favourite instance of this is this comically human account of a race between Peter and John in John 20:

> Mary Magdalene went to the tomb and saw that the stone had been removed from the entrance. So she came running to Simon Peter and the other disciple, the one Jesus loved, and said, 'They have taken the Lord out of the tomb, and we don't know where they have put him!' So Peter and the other disciple started for the tomb. Both were running, but the other disciple outran Peter and reached the tomb first.
> JOHN 20:1–4

It wasn't that he thought himself the only loved one, but rather that the fact he was loved by Jesus was the thing he most wanted people to know about him. He lived as a loved person. He was loved when he, along with everyone else, abandoned Jesus in the hour of his greatest need, on the night of his arrest. He was confident enough of this love to make his way to the foot of the cross, from where Jesus validated his belief by giving him the task of caring for his own mother. John was the disciple Jesus loved. We are those Jesus loves. Let that sink in.

For reflection

What makes it hard for you to understand or accept God's love for you? What would change if you were able to live deeply rooted and established in love?

Prayer

Lord, my mind is too dull and my heart too small to grasp your love. Please, by your Spirit, help me understand. Amen.

Sokoke scops owl *Otus ireneae*

Dakatcha – A Rocha Kenya's nature reserve of threatened woodland – offers the perfect habitat for Africa's smallest owl and twelve other species on the Red List of the International Union for Conservation of Nature (IUCN).

Day 3

Judged

Now the glory of the God of Israel went up from above the cherubim, where it had been, and moved to the threshold of the temple. Then the Lord called to the man clothed in linen who had the writing kit at his side and said to him, 'Go throughout the city of Jerusalem and put a mark on the foreheads of those who grieve and lament over all the detestable things that are done in it.'

As I listened, he said to the others, 'Follow him through the city and kill, without showing pity or compassion. Slaughter the old men, the young men and women, the mothers and children, but do not touch anyone who has the mark. Begin at my sanctuary.' So they began with the old men who were in front of the temple.

Then he said to them, 'Defile the temple and fill the courts with the slain. Go!' So they went out and began killing throughout the city. While they were killing and I was left alone, I fell face down, crying out, 'Alas, Sovereign Lord! Are you going to destroy the entire remnant of Israel in this outpouring of your wrath on Jerusalem?'

He answered me, 'The sin of the people of Israel and Judah is exceedingly great; the land is full of bloodshed and the city is full of injustice. They say, "The Lord has forsaken the land; the Lord does not see." So I will not look on them with pity or spare them, but I will bring down on their own heads what they have done.'

EZEKIEL 9:3–10

People have always judged the judgement of God. We like to think we would do a better job – sometimes harsher, sometimes more lenient. There are those who believe God shouldn't judge at all. He should affirm and accept us how we are, because he is supposed to be – in a particular understanding of the word – loving. The cross, they argue, has nothing to do with judgement. It was an act of solidarity with our suffering. God now really *gets it*.

When it comes to forming an understanding of God and how he works in the world, we can draw from various sources of authority: scripture, reason, tradition and experience. Like it or not, scripture is not ambiguous about whether God judges. Let's think about this short passage in Ezekiel to see what it tells us about what, how and who he judges.

Ezekiel was a trainee priest, only around 25 years old, when he was one of those taken into Babylonian exile. A decade later, those left in Israel once again rebelled against the occupiers and this time they were decimated. The prophets in Jerusalem, Jeremiah, Zephaniah and Habakkuk, had delivered God's warnings to deaf ears. People understood that Babylon was enacting God's judgement, but was it fair? Couldn't he have been merciful and held back his wrath so they could have a bit longer to turn things around? Weren't they his special people, in a land he had given them, with a temple in which his very glory dwelt?

It fell to Ezekiel to justify God's actions. From house arrest almost 1,000 miles away, Ezekiel is given a virtual tour of the temple back in Jerusalem. To his horror he witnesses flagrant, treacherous idol worship in this holy place of worship, with the worst societal, political and personal sin widespread in the city and beyond. The perpetrators may say, 'The Lord does not see,' (v. 9) but he does. What does God judge? In short, sin.

How does God judge? Part of this passage seems to say he is merciless and even cruel: 'I will not look on them with pity or spare them' (v. 10). But we know from the rest of scripture that God is slow to anger, full of love, a God whose very name – Yahweh – is defined as 'compassionate and gracious' (Exodus 34:6; Psalm 103:8–10; Jonah 4:2). These words would not have been spoken coldly; this judgement would have brought no pleasure. The judgement of God is above all righteous and holy, because God's actions never contradict his character.

Lastly, who does God judge? We might just about be able to stomach the idea of God judging others – those who commit extensive atrocities, for example – but how about us? How about the church and the good Christian people like me in it?

In today's passage God's judgement falls on his own special people, who professed loyalty and devotion and then, idiotically thinking they could hide what they were up to, brought idols into his house. Fierce and faithful love has no genial tolerance of betrayal. God will not be mocked and so, in fulfilment of this terrible vision, judgement would come to be enacted at the hands of the Babylonians. We who say we are God's own are all the more under his judgement when we stray: 'For it is time for judgement to begin with God's household; and if it begins with us, what will the outcome be for those who do not obey the gospel of God?' (1 Peter 4:17).

Let's end with hope. God is the same yesterday, today and forever. Evil of all kinds will always justify his judgement. And he has always offered a way for us to be spared the consequences. Here, those who grieved and lamented 'over all the detestable things' (v. 4) were passed over, as the Israelite firstborn sons were generations earlier in Egypt. And as we will be because of the cross.

For reflection

What does God's judgement of sin tell us about his character? What can be done to avoid taking his forgiveness of our wrongdoing for granted?

Prayer

Holy God, I stand before you and confess the unholy thoughts, words and actions of the recent past. I know I deserve your judgement. And I ask you to forgive me and make me clean and whole again. Thank you for your love and mercy. Amen.

European roller *Coracias garrulus*

A Rocha France has studied and protected this magnificent bird since 2002. Our findings influence new conservation measures and populations are responding positively.

Day 4

In covenant

The Lord did not set his affection on you and choose you because you were more numerous than other peoples, for you were the fewest of all peoples. But it was because the Lord loved you and kept the oath he swore to your ancestors that he brought you out with a mighty hand and redeemed you from the land of slavery, from the power of Pharaoh king of Egypt. Know therefore that the Lord your God is God; he is the faithful God, keeping his covenant of love to a thousand generations of those who love him and keep his commandments. But

> **those who hate him he will repay to their face by destruction;
> he will not be slow to repay to their face those who hate him.**

Therefore, take care to follow the commands, decrees and laws I give you today.
DEUTERONOMY 7:7–11

'How was school today?'

'Great – we renewed our covenant with the teachers and did the ink ceremony. Hope you have that new washing powder. It got all over my shirt.'

That's not a conversation you are likely to have with a young person in your life, and not just because there is little chance that you know a teenager who is concerned about getting stains out. The only place the word 'covenant' remains in circulation today is in relation to marriage, so if you are blurry about its meaning you won't be alone. But God chose this form of commitment to define his relationship with individuals, a people, a nation and ultimately all the earth, so it is worth giving time to understand it.

Simply put, a covenant is a binding agreement between two parties, involving obligations and commitments. It is often associated with oaths, signs and ceremonies: think 'Till death us do part', the exchanging of rings, the drinking of toasts. It is far more personal and relational than a contract, though it is similarly binding and serious.

The Bible records God entering five covenants. We will be coming back to the first, in the time of Noah, in a few days' time. The second was with Abraham, an elderly childless nomad, to whom God promised land, descendants and blessing – all of which he delivered. The third came to Moses: laws to set a people apart to be his own. This covenant came with clear consequences: keep the law and be blessed; break it and be cursed. Those are the covenants in place at the time of this Deuteronomy passage. The fourth was to David – one of his descendants would take a forever-throne. And the fifth and last was foretold by the prophet Jeremiah (Jeremiah 31:31–34) and was inaugurated by the death of Jesus – Jesus, who, by the way, was in the line of David. God does what he says.

That God chose to set covenantal terms with creation tells us so much about our creator. There are, after all, other approaches he could have taken. He could have defined the relationship in purely hierarchical terms, putting us in our place a very long way beneath him. He could have completely ignored us. He could have gone the legal route, holding us to our obligations without mercy. There are rulers of kingdoms large and small who relate in just that way to subordinates. My brother was once given a parking ticket as he lay bleeding on the ground next to his crashed (thus illegally stopped) moped. This parking attendant was enjoying his power rather a lot.

Take a minute to read our passage again, focusing this time on the verbs associated with God here.

What struck you? When I did this, I was hit between the eyes by love: extravagant, undeserved, faithful, costly love. God is the instigator of this relationship. He loves first and he loves best. Out of love he swears oaths and holds to them. And then because he loves us, he is not remotely indifferent to our response. There is an intensity and depth here that any spurned lover will recognise: 'Those who hate him he will repay to their face by destruction' (v. 10). If a woman scorned is hellishly furious, as Shakespeare had it, how much more so the Lord Almighty?

This is a frightening situation if you think about it, because which of us gives God the love he deserves? The Israelites certainly didn't. The cycle of failure, repentance and mercy wraps the history of God's people in chains that could have bound them forever. No sacrificial goat, grain or gold was ever going to be enough to atone for their stone-cold hearts.

And so we come to a Passover supper in an upper room in Jerusalem. The faithfulness of God has led here, and his love is about to take him straight into the jaws of death. Jesus takes the wine and says, 'This cup is the new covenant in my blood, which is poured out for you' (Luke 22:20). This new covenant makes Jesus the mediator of the relationship between us and God. Those 'commands, decrees and laws' are no longer covenant conditions and the destruction we deserve isn't a covenant consequence. What binds us now is pure grace.

For reflection

'Know therefore that the Lord your God is God; he is the faithful God, keeping his covenant of love to a thousand generations' (v. 9). How do you see God keeping his covenant in your generation?

Prayer

Lord God, you owed us nothing and yet you chose to make promises to save us and bless us. Thank you for being willing to do whatever it took for us to be in relationship with you. Amen.

Horseshoe crab *Limulus polyphemus*

This ancient creature is under threat due to factors such as shoreline development and nutrient runoff. A Rocha USA is part of monitoring their well-being to learn how to help.

Day 5

Understood

Nothing in all creation is hidden from God's sight. Everything is uncovered and laid bare before the eyes of him to whom we must give account.

Therefore, since we have a great high priest who has ascended into heaven, Jesus the Son of God, let us hold firmly to the faith we profess. For we do not have a high priest who is unable to feel sympathy for our weaknesses, but we have one who has been tempted in every way, just as we are – yet he did not sin. Let us then approach God's throne of grace with confidence, so that we may receive mercy and find grace to help us in our time of need.
HEBREWS 4:13–16

People quite enjoy judging each other, because in putting someone down we feel we are elevated by default to a superior position. Two doors down from where I live there is a family with a dog who spends most of its time in the front garden barking through the gate. The barking drives me up the wall, and I'll admit that I judge that dog's owners. I've never had a dog, but if I had one I would never let it become a public nuisance like that.

However, you will never catch me judging a parent of a toddler having a meltdown in the Tesco ice cream aisle or deciding to wear the ice cream no responsible parent would have bought them rather than eating it. I understand that sometimes you have to negotiate with tiny terrorists, because I've been there.

You may never have heard of the 19th-century American temperance reformer, suffragist and poet Mary T. Lathrap, but it is likely you are familiar with a phrase from one of her poems, 'Judge softly',[5] which begins:

Pray, don't find fault with the man that limps,
Or stumbles along the road.
Unless you have worn the moccasins he wears,
Or stumbled beneath the same load.

We've been exploring how the death and resurrection of Jesus changed humanity's relationship with God. That Jesus died was only possible because he 'took frail flesh'.[6] He was born a man and for 33 years lived with the same physical limitations of any other man. But not only this, he was subject to the same temptations. By the time he submitted to the hammer and nails of his executioners, he was fully aware of our weakness, our suffering and why we so very, very often fail to make the righteous and holy choices. In other words, he had gone a mile in our moccasins and then some.

The book of Hebrews had a primarily Jewish audience. The first of the ten commandments couldn't have been clearer: no other gods! So Hebrews begins by setting out the divinity of Christ and his unity with God the Father. Jesus is God's voice to us, the means by which he created the universe, the 'radiance of God's glory and the exact representation of his being' (1:3). The people of Israel knew the radiance of God's glory to be terrifying enough to throw a person to the ground, to dazzle sight and cause deathly fear. The structure of their temple emphasised the danger of the holiness of God to an ordinary person, as did the sacrificial system, the priesthood and the stories of what happened to those who stumbled with the ark of the covenant, offered strange fire or made fun of a prophet's bald head (2 Samuel 6:6–7; Leviticus 10:1–3; 2 Kings 2:23–24). In Jesus, God's glory was fully present but approachable. As the one to provide 'purification for sins', Hebrews explains (1:3), it was fitting for him to share in our humanity:

'He had to be made like them, fully human in every way, in order that he might become a merciful and faithful high priest' (2:17).

There are some dreams that most of us seem to have had at some point: the one where you suddenly realise you are naked in public, and the one where you stand up to give a speech or sit down to do an exam and have absolutely nothing to say. These dreams are about exposure, about being unable to hide the truth of who you are. There is a day coming when that experience won't be one from which we awake, a day when we stand before God with absolutely nowhere to hide. Hebrews 4:13 could very well be the nightmare to end all nightmares, were that where everything ended. But it isn't. We can have full confidence that we'll 'receive mercy and find grace' (v. 16) because Jesus is our high priest.

In Judaism, a high priest was the only one allowed to enter the Holy of Holies in the Jerusalem temple, and that only once a year. On Yom Kippur, the Day of Atonement, he would enter this inner sanctum to burn incense and sprinkle sacrificial animal blood for the expiation of his own sins and those of the people of Israel. Jesus had no sin and was therefore able to *be the sacrifice*. And not only that, but he also understood in his bones those in need of purifying.

For reflection

Have you experienced the benefits of someone in power over you having direct experience of your situation in a way that has made them empathetic? For example, I had a boss who was also a mother, who was very compassionate towards me when I went back to work after maternity leave. What light can your experience shed on why it was so important that Jesus save us as one of us?

Prayer

When we come to you, God, the judge of all, thank you that we also come to Jesus, the mediator of a new covenant. We worship you now, with reverence and awe, so grateful that we can come close without fear, assured of your loving welcome (from Hebrews 12:18–28).

Indian elephant *Elephas maximus indicus*

A Rocha India is helping solve the growing issue of human–elephant conflict in and around Bannerghatta National Park.

Day 6

Being saved

For Christ did not send me to baptise, but to preach the gospel – not with wisdom and eloquence, lest the cross of Christ be emptied of its power.

For the message of the cross is foolishness to those who are perishing, but to us who are being saved it is the power of God. For it is written:

> 'I will destroy the wisdom of the wise;
> the intelligence of the intelligent I will frustrate.'

Where is the wise person? Where is the teacher of the law? Where is the philosopher of this age? Has not God made foolish the wisdom of the world? For since in the wisdom of God the world through its wisdom did not know him, God was pleased through the foolishness of what was preached to save those who believe. Jews demand signs and Greeks look for wisdom, but we preach Christ crucified: a stumbling-block to Jews and foolishness to Gentiles, but to those whom God has called, both Jews and Greeks, Christ the power of God and the wisdom of God.

1 CORINTHIANS 1:17–24

The cross of Christ can change people from 'those who are perishing' to 'those who are being saved.' So far, so familiar. But also, so very hard to get your head around. Or my head anyway. Let's break it down to the component parts: cross, Christ, perishing, saved.

This short extract from one of Paul's letters to the Corinthian church highlights just how different the *cross* looks depending on where you are standing. It has power (vv. 17–18) but can seem to some like utter foolishness (vv. 18, 21, 23). It is a stumbling block (v. 23) and the wisdom of God (v. 24). Let's remind ourselves of the bare facts. Crucifixion was a form of execution probably invented by the Assyrians and Babylonians and introduced to Rome in the 3rd century BC. It was rarely used on Roman citizens, instead largely reserved for slaves, foreigners and disgraced soldiers, and after Jesus, Christians. The victim would be stripped naked and nailed through hands and feet to intersecting beams of wood, then raised to a vertical position, where they would hang until they died of haemorrhage, dehydration, shock, asphyxia or cardiac arrest. Not only was this form of death gruesome and agonising in the extreme, but it was imbued with shame. The idea that we should worship someone who died *in this particular way* is shocking. The only reason we might not be shocked by it is that there are now crosses in Christian places of worship all around the world as well as everywhere from necklaces to bumper stickers.

Next, *Christ*. Paul says that Christ is 'the power of God and the wisdom of God' (v. 24). John's account of Jesus' life opens with the reality that although he is creator and ruler of the world, he was and still is not – by and large – received or recognised as such (John 1:9–11). Research carried out in the UK in 2022 showed 25% of respondents believed Jesus was an ordinary human, with a further 33% agreeing with the statement that he was a prophet or spiritual leader, but not God.[7] It requires a leap of faith to think that anything relating to a man who lived in Palestine in the first century might impact our status before God.

Now we come to the idea of *perishing*. To perish is to die, but Paul is clearly not thinking of the death that comes to us all, because he speaks about two groups here – the perishing ones and the ones being saved. The 'perishing' are on a trajectory of destruction leading to terminal disaster; they are too 'wise' in a worldly sense to accept God's means of rescue. To such people 'the message of the cross is foolishness' (v. 18). This tweeter is here to explain the real reason Jesus died on the cross:

> @masonmennenga: 'Jesus didn't die for your sins. He died because he was a poor brown revolutionary that was a threat to the Roman Empire.'

Oh – silly us! Thanks for clearing that up @masonmennenga. In answer to Paul's question, 'Where is the philosopher of this age?' (v. 20): in this age, you can find him on X.

And so to the last part: *saved*. The foolish, outrageous proposition of Christianity is that by believing that Jesus is God and that his execution by crucifixion has absolved us of the death penalty we deserve for our sin, we are saved from death. The life we live now has no end, only alteration. I don't understand it, but neither do I understand long division, the scale of the universe, how voices are carried between mobile phones or multiverse theory. Faith is a gift. It requires the humility to accept the limitations of our intelligence (v. 19) and the uncomfortable truth that without God's intervention, we face death. And then the Holy Spirit can open our eyes and enable us to see the glory of the cross and the son of God hung there, for our salvation.

For reflection

Are you demanding signs or looking for wisdom? Try to be really honest about this. I guess most of us do these things at least some of the time. Tell God you are sorry and ask for his help to rely only on his power, and to be satisfied by his wisdom, however foolish it seems to the perishing.

Prayer

Lord, I believe. Help my unbelief (from Mark 9:24).

White-naped mangabey *Cercocebus lunulatus*

A Rocha camera traps confirmed the presence of this monkey in the Atewa Forest in 2017, the first photo ever taken of this species in Ghana.

Day 7

Forgiven

This is the message we have heard from him and declare to you: God is light; in him there is no darkness at all. If we claim to have fellowship with him and yet walk in the darkness, we lie and do not live out the truth. But if we walk in the light, as he is in the light, we have fellowship with one another, and the blood of Jesus, his Son, purifies us from all sin.

If we claim to be without sin, we deceive ourselves and the truth is not in us. If we confess our sins, he is faithful and just and will forgive us our sins and purify us from all unrighteousness. If we claim we have not sinned, we make him out to be a liar and his word is not in us.
1 JOHN 1:5–10

I spent most of my childhood in Portugal, in A Rocha's first field study centre. Lots of people came and went, some staying a few days, some for years. There were birds, moths, rare orchids and a bunch of motley pets, almond orchards and vineyards, plenty of company if you needed it.

It was a very colourful setting, and I'm grateful for many aspects of my upbringing, but one thing that was hard was being the only Christian at my school other than my siblings. By the age of 11 I was wondering if my faith was strong enough to justify all the teasing it generated from my peers. I toyed with the idea of quietly letting the whole thing drift off my radar.

That summer, a group of students visited and invited me to join them on a beach trip one day. We swam and sunbathed and then they prayed for me to be filled with the Holy Spirit. The Holy Spirit filled me! It was a life-altering experience and set me on a trajectory I'm still following. In my newfound passion for Jesus, I read the Bible, prayed and evangelised to all and sundry, including my long-suffering parents, who I felt had become rather lukewarm and needed a shake-up.

Not long into what became semi-affectionately referred to as my 'Holy Jo phase', my mum asked me to do the washing up and I had a major, messy strop. In the aftermath of the incident, she found me glowering angrily in my bedroom and said something along the lines of, 'It is all very well you talking about how much you love God, but it doesn't mean a lot if you are going to be a rotter when you are asked to help out.' Ouch. I was mortified. She had a point, a sharp one, and I felt it. In the terminology of our reading from 1 John, I was claiming to have fellowship with God, but my actions contradicted my words.

There's a flaw with my illustration, though, which I need you to catch. John is not saying we can't say we are Christians unless our lives are perfect. He says the 'blood of Jesus… purifies us from all sin' (v. 7), so clearly there is still sin around, and Jesus is the one to deal with it, not us. This is about walking. Walking is purposeful. It is not a single step but one after another after another. Walking is John's metaphor for a way of life, a way of being, a pattern of behaviour. The first thing for us to grasp about what John is saying about forgiveness here is that it is for those who in a general sense are 'walking in the light'. Is God's forgiveness of sin conditional? Well, yes, in a way it is.

The next paragraph, verses 8 to 10, throw another condition in the mix. We can't be forgiven if we think we have done nothing wrong. I have heard people express a wide range of reasons for rejecting the gospel, everything from the problem of evil to the existence of other religions to a belief that science contradicts faith. And I have one friend who says her issue is that she feels she is a very good person. Not only does she contend that she has no sins to declare, but she feels she should get credit for how great she is. The Christian message doesn't work for her at all.

The first of Alcoholic Anonymous' twelve steps is: 'We admitted we were powerless over alcohol – that our lives had become unmanageable.'[8] Before recovery is possible, there must be a reckoning with reality, however painful and ugly that reality might be. John's argument here is the same: in itself, sin is not the problem. God knows 'we are dust' (Psalm 103:14). Why else would he have resorted to becoming man and making himself the ultimate sacrifice?

Only denial of sin can hinder God's forgiveness. We need to resist that urge to cover up and hide that we've had since Adam and Eve ate the forbidden fruit and step into the blazing light of God's holiness. There is nothing we could ever do that makes us so dirty God can't make us sparkly clean. This is the gift of the cross.

For reflection

We are very good at deceiving ourselves. Here is an opportunity to look unflinchingly at the truth. What are you covering up? What are you afraid to see in yourself? Remember that you are safe in God's love and confess to him what you discover.

Prayer

> *Heavenly Father, You have searched me and you know me. I can't hide any part of who I am from your sight. Sometimes I wish I could! But when you look at me you see someone you love completely and utterly, so help me come close. Help me accept your kindness. Amen.*

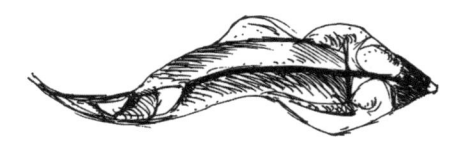

Halavi guitarfish *Glaucostegus halavi*

Guitarfish, sharks and rays are under enormous threat globally. A Rocha monitors their populations off the Kenyan coast to identify key habitats and nursery areas.

Day 8

Reconciled

As for you, you were dead in your transgressions and sins, in which you used to live when you followed the ways of this world and of the ruler of the kingdom of the air, the spirit who is now at work in those who are disobedient. All of us also lived among them at one time, gratifying the cravings of our flesh and following its desires and thoughts. Like the rest, we were by nature deserving of wrath. But because of his great love for us, God, who is rich in mercy, made us alive with Christ even when we were dead in transgressions – it is by grace you have been saved. And God raised us up with Christ and seated us with him in the heavenly realms in Christ Jesus, in order that in the coming ages he might show the incomparable riches of his grace, expressed in his kindness to us in Christ Jesus. For it is by grace you have been saved, through faith – and this is not from yourselves, it is the gift of God – not by works, so that no one can boast. For we are God's handiwork, created in Christ Jesus to do good works, which God prepared in advance for us to do.
EPHESIANS 2:1–10

Some parts of the Bible are obscure, to say the least. What are we to make of the interbreeding of men and angels in Genesis, or the talking donkey in Numbers, or the four eye-encrusted creatures around the throne in Revelation? Genres like apocalyptic literature have fallen out of use and a vast chasm of time and culture lies between us and Old Testament historical narrative. But perhaps more surprising than finding some parts of scripture hard to interpret is the clear and plain meaning of the New Testament letters. While they still require diligent and careful reading, understanding of their context and so on, they are remarkably accessible to us, here and now.

Our reading today is an extract from a letter to the early church in Ephesus, in what is now Turkey. Without the context of Judaism, the Ephesian church needed simple and plain explanations of concepts such as sin and separation from God and of ways reconciliation could be accomplished. We then are blessed to have this help in understanding God's 'kindness to us in Christ Jesus' too (v. 7). What did the death and resurrection of Jesus mean for our relationship with God? Well, let's look at what this letter says about that.

As we all know, conversion is seldom a simple and clean line a person steps over; more often it is a messy process during which it is all but impossible to identify a key moment where the spiritual reality shifts. However, to make his points clear, Paul sets out a dichotomy: people before and after they are saved.

Paul tells this group of believers that they used to be dead (vv. 1, 5). They followed a 'ruler', a 'spirit' who we can understand to be the Satan referred to elsewhere in the Bible.[9] They also followed 'the ways of this world' (v. 2). Much like today, in first-century Ephesus this largely entailed satisfying cravings and setting their compasses with self as True North. Twenty-first century life in some parts of the world, including mine, places the individual on the throne. We should trust our gut, put ourselves first, reach for our dreams and not worry too much about anything or anyone else. This, according to Ephesians, is more than a matter of behaviour, it is intrinsically woven into our identity. In this 'before' state we are 'by nature deserving of wrath' (v. 3).

By contrast, because of what Christ did on the cross, the saved are alive. Their spiritual reality is now that they are – present tense – resurrected from death and alive with him in the 'heavenly realms' (v. 6). These realms are not a physical place but a dimension of reality in which we live in the here and now. One day there will be no veil between us and this dimension, and what we call 'heaven' will have God living fully among us in a renewed heaven and earth.[10]

In case anyone was tempted to think they could take credit for the changed situation, Paul puts heavy emphasis on the fact this is *all* God's doing. God 'made us alive' (v. 5). God 'raised us up' (v. 6). And if that wasn't blunt enough: 'this is not from yourselves, it is the gift of God— not by works, so that no one can boast' (vv. 8–9). We don't get away from the idea of works, mind you; it is just that those works don't have a bearing on our salvation. We don't even come up with our own works – God prepares them for us.

Now and then I hear people talking about the cross as though it were all about God's judgement and hatred of sin. This passage reminds us that what took Jesus to death and beyond was great love, rich mercy, grace and kindness.

For reflection

Read the passage again, slowly. What word or phrase struck you the most? What might God want you to hear about who he is and who you are? Take a few minutes to be quiet in a posture of openness and receptivity to the Holy Spirit.

Prayer

Holy God, your love, mercy, grace and kindness towards me is undeserved and I am so, so grateful. Thank you that with your Son, I live now and forever. Thank you that I am not left to mindlessly follow my cravings but have good things to do for you in each day. Thank you that I am yours. Amen.

European storm petrel *Hydrobates pelagicus*

A Rocha Portugal has been studying these smallest of all seabirds since 1990, making it possible to examine links between climate change, oceanography, marine food webs, and the diet and migration strategies of storm petrels.

Day 9

Renewed

So I tell you this, and insist on it in the Lord, that you must no longer live as the Gentiles do, in the futility of their thinking. They are darkened in their understanding and separated from the life of God because of the ignorance that is in them due to the hardening of their hearts. Having lost all sensitivity, they have given themselves over to sensuality so as to indulge in every kind of impurity, and they are full of greed.

That, however, is not the way of life you learned when you heard about Christ and were taught in him in accordance with the truth that is in Jesus. You were taught, with regard to your former way of life, to put off your old self, which is being corrupted by its deceitful desires; to be made new in the attitude of your minds; and to put on the new self, created to be like God in true righteousness and holiness.
EPHESIANS 4:17–24

Shawn was raised in the south suburbs of Minneapolis, USA, around substance abuse, domestic violence and crime. He learnt early on that he needed to look after himself. Sometimes this meant finding paid work so that he could get toothpaste and food or knowing where to hide if a situation turned dangerous. The few photographs of him as a child show wide, wary eyes, slightly wild hair, a haunted expression. As he hit his teenage years, self-care meant joining a gang, drinking heavily and raising his fists often enough to earn himself the nickname Scrappy. He was bright but demotivated, and he coasted through high school making no effort academically. He often took reckless risks with his own life. We'll come back to Shawn later.

We are in Ephesians again today, and still in the realm of contrast. The word 'Gentiles' here is not used in quite the same way as it usually would be, referring to a non-Jew, but rather to mean those who have not accepted Christ. Gentiles and those 'in Christ' (what we'd now call Christians) are described here as profoundly different in many regards.

As we continue to reflect on what the cross means for the relationship between humanity and God, let's turn our attention to the change that happens in a person as they begin to live a forgiven life in close relationship with Christ. As with the rest of creation, God doesn't see us as lost causes who need to be blitzed into oblivion and remade from scratch. He loved us before we loved him. He loves those who are lost and have no desire to be found. In relationship with him we are *re*newed, not 'newed' (think I made up a new word there!). That said, there are definitely changes that happen in a person who once was 'separated from the life of God' (v. 18) and is no longer.

Cognitive behavioural therapy works with what is known as the cognitive triangle of thoughts, feelings and behaviour. This model emphasises the impact of thoughts on feelings and feelings on behaviour, and focuses intervention on thought as the point in the triangle over which we have the greatest agency. Paul seems to work on the same assumption. He locates much of the problem of the 'Gentiles' in their minds, describing their thinking as futile and their understanding as darkened. Their hearts then are 'hardened' and as a result their behaviour is, as it is rather delicately put, 'impure'. When it comes to turning things around, once again he starts in the realm of conscious thought: 'Be made new in the attitude of your *minds*' (v. 23, emphasis mine). Renewed thinking in turn transforms feelings and behaviour. The new self is transformed into what it was always supposed to be: righteous and holy, like God.

Back to Shawn, who we left heading down a path of destruction at the age of 17. He might have continued on his trajectory were it not for two events. The first was a car crash in which he cheated death by the skin of his teeth and which led him to pray that God would show himself. The second was that his friend broke up with a Christian girl, who Shawn then asked out and who took him to church, where the Holy Spirit met him.

Shawn is my husband. He is a profoundly good man, someone of increasing righteousness and holiness. Unlike me, he has an extremely calm and even disposition, no hint in him of the angry, scrappy young man he once was. In relationship with his Father God, his mind sharpened and he applied it, studying the Bible first in an undergraduate setting, then at master's level and then in training for ordination in the Church of England. Shawn is the best example I know of someone who put off his old self and put on his God-shaped new one. I gather from him and others who knew him then that at his conversion the change was instantaneous and dramatic. I can testify that it continues. He is someone God is renewing all the time. May it be so for me, and for you too.

For reflection

The imperatives to 'put off' our old self and 'put on' our new self imply that we need to be actively involved in the process of changing into the likeness of Christ. What are you doing to help you live as your new self? What habits or disciplines do you have in place to support your growth into righteousness and holiness? Are there any that might be helpful to add into the mix?

Prayer

Thank you, Lord God, that your love for me is not dependent on my way of life. Help me show love back to you by living in the way you intended, and becoming the person I was created to be, someone very like you. Amen.

Oregon forestsnail *Allogona townsendiana*

This terrestrial snail is endemic to the Pacific Northwest. A Rocha Canada has monitored a small population in the Little Campbell River watershed (British Columbia) since 2013 to observe and mitigate any potential impacts to the population and habitat.

Day 10

Made eternal

'I have spoken to you of earthly things and you do not believe; how then will you believe if I speak of heavenly things? No one has ever gone into heaven except the one who came from heaven – the Son of Man. Just as Moses lifted up the snake in the wilderness, so the Son of Man must be lifted up, that everyone who believes may have eternal life in him.'
   For God so loved the world that he gave his one and only Son, that whoever believes in him shall not perish but have eternal life. For God did not send his Son into the world to condemn the world, but to save the world through him. Whoever believes in him is not condemned, but whoever does not believe stands condemned already because they have not believed in the name of God's one and only Son. This is the verdict: light has come into the world, but people loved darkness instead of light because their deeds were evil.
JOHN 3:12–19

The American statesman Benjamin Franklin famously once said, 'In this world, nothing can be said to be certain, except death and taxes.' But just as people seem intent on finding tax loopholes, so we attempt to live in denial of our mortality. Whether we ignore or actively fight it, few have made peace with the notion of an expiry date. Death may come to us all, but far from seeing it as a natural part of the created order, we find it repugnant, horrifying and tragic. In 1 Corinthians, Paul calls it 'the last enemy' (15:26).

This part of John's gospel captures an interaction between Jesus and a senior Jewish leader, Nicodemus. Nicodemus is doing his best to figure out how Jesus fits into his religious world view, and he's curious enough to risk a meeting, albeit under cover of darkness. While his presenting question seems to be whether Jesus is on God's side, Jesus answers his real question, the one he didn't vocalise: 'How can I enter the kingdom of God?' Or in other words, can you save me from my inevitable death? Don't we all resonate with this heart cry? Save us and those we love! Don't let us die; we want to live!

This is where Jesus first speaks about a second birth. Nicodemus, bless him, wonders aloud how he's supposed to climb back inside his mother. I'm always grateful to anyone willing to ask the stupid question we are all thinking. Jesus explains that the first birth is of our flesh; we enter the world via our mother's womb. The second birth is of the Spirit. Those born of the Spirit are born into a life in the kingdom where they will be alive forever.

Let's pause here for just a minute to make sure we don't get in a tangle later. In the way we use language now, we could easily mishear and think Jesus means our first birth is physical and our second an entry into an ethereal, disembodied floaty life. Jesus was resurrected in his body. All the biblical language around our future selves points to more solid, hardier, enduring bodies: we can expect to go from tents to buildings, seeds to trees, naked to clothed, decaying to glorified. This world is *good*, and Jesus came to save it, not condemn it.

For ten days we've been looking at how the cross changed things for humanity. Here is where things get metaphysical. By being 'lifted up' – literally cranked into the vertical position while nailed to planks of wood, and thereafter lifted up from the grave – Jesus the 'Son of Man' changes the fundamental essence of those who believe in him from mortal to immortal. This is both very simple and appealing and at the same time confusing and uninviting, if you happen to 'love darkness'. John introduces the language of light and darkness in the first chapter of his gospel, along with the observation that not everyone prefers light. Few would tick the 'No' box on a survey asking, 'If you could avoid death, would you?' But plenty would if the question included reference to the need to believe in Christ and giving up a life of evil deeds. The truth is some choose to perish. Some choose condemnation.

And others believe and choose life. The love of God, expressed in the self-giving sacrifice of his Son Jesus, has the power to mean death does not have to be the end. Like Nicodemus, I have many stupid questions of a logistical nature, things like where are we in the gap between our dead bodies decomposing and getting our new ones? Will the world have to be recreated a very different size to accommodate everyone? Will everyone be the same age as each other? Will we recognise those we knew in this life? I don't expect Jesus to send me answers on a postcard. But I do expect him to be true to his word that I will go through death and out the other side, thanks to his kindness, mercy, faithfulness and great love.

For reflection

Take some time to think about your own death. What feelings do you have about it? How does your death affect the way you live? Have you done any preparations or had any conversations with loved ones about dying? Why or why not?

Prayer

God, who is life and light and love, I give you my grief and my fears about death. You understand them. You descended to death and rose to life to open the way for us to follow. I believe. I believe and I choose to follow you into a life in your kingdom that will not end. Amen.

Tiger *Panthera tigris*

In 2015, A Rocha India scientists tracked a solitary male tiger roaming Bannerghatta Park, where A Rocha is based. He has now established his territory. Recently a female was recorded in the area – perhaps this will lead to a breeding population.

II

God and creation

WHAT ARE WE DOING spending ten days of Lent thinking about 'the world, and all who live in it' (Psalm 24:1)? Having grown up associated with A Rocha, I have heard many objections expressed about Christians devoting time and resources to anything other than preaching Paul's distillation of the gospel in 1 Corinthians 15:3–4: 'Christ died for our sins according to the Scriptures, that he was buried, that he was raised on the third day according to the Scriptures.' Christians should not, according to some, waste effort on tracking bird migration, digging out invasive species of cactus or campaigning to protect virgin forest, because none of this is what they would define as a 'gospel' matter.

Paul preached the gospel in a variety of ways, however, depending on the context. Acts 17 begins with an account of his approach when explaining the cross to a Jewish audience. His message weaves around Old Testament texts which found their fulfilment in Jesus. Later in the same chapter, he's speaking to the multicultural citizens of Athens, and he starts with creation:

> The God who made the world and everything in it is the Lord of heaven and earth and does not live in temples built by human hands. And he is not served by human hands, as if he needed anything. Rather, he himself gives everyone life and breath and everything else.
> ACTS 17:24–25

In his commentary on these speeches, John Stott writes:

> Many people are rejecting our gospel today not because they perceive it to be false, but because they perceive it to be trivial. People are looking for an integrated worldview which makes sense of all their experience. We learn from Paul that we cannot preach the gospel of Jesus without the doctrine of God, or the cross without the creation.[11]

The gospel – the good news – of Jesus is both simple and more beautifully complex than the universe. It is piercingly specific and expansive enough to encompass everything. It is about the cross and the resurrection, and a Messiah whose love and commitment is for me, for you and, yes, for *all things*.

Day 11

Whose world is it?

> Who is like you, Lord God Almighty?
>   You, Lord, are mighty, and your faithfulness surrounds you.
> You rule over the surging sea;
>   when its waves mount up, you still them.
> You crushed Rahab like one of the slain;
>   with your strong arm you scattered your enemies.
> The heavens are yours, and yours also the earth;
>   you founded the world and all that is in it.
> You created the north and the south;
>   Tabor and Hermon sing for joy at your name.
> Your arm is endowed with power;
>   your hand is strong, your right hand exalted.
>
> PSALM 89:8–13

My favourite museum in the world is Edinburgh's World of Illusions. It has a vortex tunnel, mirror maze, colour shadow wall and, best of all, a room which can shrink and grow you. It actually can – I saw it with my very own eyes and have a photograph of my daughters, one miniscule and one giant, to prove it.

But, of course, our eyes can deceive us, sometimes to entertaining effect, and our brains are not entirely reliable interpreters of reality. One of the illusions to which we are most susceptible is the impression that the world belongs to humans. We use language like natural resources and ecosystem services. Our governments have land registries where they record 'ownership'. Countries wrangle over fishing rights. Some nations have the audacity to march down the road and annexe territory that 'belonged' to another nation.

Living under this illusion has had devastating consequences. Believing the world and all that is in it belongs to us, we have taken the liberty of using it to fulfil our desires for more, faster, cheaper stuff. We have both consumed the goodness of the soil, the air and the water and used them to dump our toxic trash. In 2021 we generated 460 million metric tonnes of plastic waste globally, around 40% of which went into the sea.[12] Bird populations are in freefall: there are a billion fewer of our feathered friends in the USA alone than there were 50 years ago. Our summers are becoming dangerously hot because we've generated so much greenhouse gas it's like the atmosphere is wrapped in five chunky wool sweaters and a fleecy blanket when it only needs a cotton throw. But that's fine – we can turn on the air con and dig a few more chlorinated swimming pools. We might not want to swim in a river or lake, though, because the toxins we've dumped could make us sick. If we think all of it is ours, we believe we have the right to do what we want with it even if that's to utterly trash the place.

As Christians we need to take off the sight-warping glasses worn by the rest of the world and see the truth. In the words of Psalm 24:1, 'The earth is the Lord's, and everything in it, the world, and all who live in it.' Today's reading from Psalm 89 was composed by a poetic soul who may not have had a particularly scientific understanding of how things work but who captures the essence of reality with majestic clarity. The vast scope of the universe – space with its planets, moons, asteroids and comets (the 'heavens'), and the earth (our tiny bit of the universe) – belongs to God (v. 11). He did not transfer ownership and go off to do something else. He 'rules' over the sea, he 'stills' the waves, he 'crushes' and 'scatters' his enemies. He is, the psalmist tells us, mighty, faithful, strong and powerful. It is mind-blowing to think how casually we mistreat his highly valued, much-loved world.

Did God create humans in his image and love us so much he sent his Son to die for us? Yes. Does he love only us? Let Jesus answer that: 'For God so loved *the world* that he gave his only Son' (John 3:16, emphasis mine). The English word 'world' here is translated from the Greek *Kosmos*, from which we get 'cosmos', meaning the whole universe.

John begins his gospel before anything other than God existed and then immediately puts Jesus in relationship with 'all things' (John 1:3).

We've been thinking at a scale that is in danger of making this all seem rather abstract, so let me take it down to a more relatable level by telling you about my friend Megan. Megan has a guinea pig who she holds in higher regard than many people hold their spouses. Ruffus is her pride and joy, the subject of 90% of her social media posts, owner of a large array of toys, and wearer of diverse costumes for occasions such as royal weddings and birthdays. While Megan would rather not leave Ruffus' tuffty side, now and then she goes on holidays to places Ruffus is not welcome. Megan is someone I love very much. If she trusts me enough to choose me as Ruffus' guardian in her absence, am I going to give him to my cats for a bit of bloody entertainment? Am I going to forget to feed him or feed him something I know will give him a sore tummy? Not if I care even a little bit about my relationship with Megan.

For reflection

What would someone deduce about how I feel towards God based on the way I live in his world?

Prayer

Lord God, I have a very long way to go in living with integrity – such that my behaviour echoes my words of praise and devotion to you. Thank you for your long-suffering patience and grace. I receive your forgiveness, and I promise to keep striving for holiness. Amen.

Tree frog *Hyla savignyi*

The tree frog loves to climb – usually on twigs or leaves but pencils will do! This one did so in the Bekaa Valley in Lebanon.

Day 12

Under his command

'Who cuts a channel for the torrents of rain,
    and a path for the thunderstorm,
to water a land where no one lives,
    an uninhabited desert,
to satisfy a desolate wasteland
    and make it sprout with grass?
Does the rain have a father?
    Who fathers the drops of dew?
From whose womb comes the ice?
    Who gives birth to the frost from the heavens
when the waters become hard as stone,
    when the surface of the deep is frozen?

'Can you bind the chains of the Pleiades?
    Can you loosen Orion's belt?
Can you bring forth the constellations in their seasons
    or lead out the Bear with its cubs?
Do you know the laws of the heavens?
    Can you set up God's dominion over the earth?

'Can you raise your voice to the clouds
    and cover yourself with a flood of water?
Do you send the lightning bolts on their way?
    Do they report to you, "Here we are"?'

JOB 38:25–35

To date the United States Air Force has carried out over 1,500 weather modification experiments, with outlandish names like Project Stardust, Operation Popeye and Project Stormfury. Ever since humans came up with the idea for the Tower of Babel (see Genesis 11:1–9), we've overestimated our power and the extent of our influence. Someone somewhere is probably working on a way to manoeuvre the planetary pathways to our advantage as I write. Movie makers can produce the illusion of a heavy rain shower and Project Cirrus is investigating if spraying particles into the stratosphere will induce cloud droplets to become raindrops. Those of us who have lived through another so-called summer in the UK are probably less excited about that particular experiment!

The questions in God's soliloquy are a sharp reminder to Job of who has the real power and control in this universe. For 37 chapters, Job's wife and friends have had the audacity to speak on God's behalf, as though his terrible trials were no mystery at all and his way ahead simple and clear. Eliphaz, Bildad and Zophar draw a straight line between Job's sin and his skin boils, bereavement and loss of livelihood. They are therefore able to give him a simple way to reverse his catastrophic losses: 'If I were you, I would appeal to God' (5:8), and then, hey presto: 'You will laugh at destruction and famine' (5:22). Bildad helpfully reminds Job that all mortals are but maggots (25:6), so he shouldn't feel he's the only one getting it wrong.

The problem is this is all nonsense. Right at the outset, we are told Job was 'blameless and upright; he feared God and shunned evil' (1:1).

One of the ways we overstretch is in our attempts to understand and assign meaning to our suffering. If we can figure out its cause, we think we can figure out how to avoid it in future. God's reply to Job is a whirlwind of such force it blows away any such idea in a heartbeat. He points Job to the wonderous, majestic, glorious creation in which he delights, and Job sees and hears what he is supposed to: something of God's very nature.

The wild, natural world is terrifying and easily overwhelms us. Earthquakes, volcanoes, thunderstorms, hungry carnivorous mammals, flash floods, burning heat – none of these can we do much, if anything, to tame. When Jesus walked on water and calmed the storm, he was in effect telling his disciples: 'I am God.' He is the God who divided land from water, who set our planet amid whole galaxies, whose word created all our somethings from nothing. In all this we have a privileged position of significance as his image bearers. But let's not get too big for our boots. He is God and we are not:

> 'For my thoughts are not your thoughts,
> neither are your ways my ways,'
> declares the Lord.
> 'As the heavens are higher than the earth,
> so are my ways higher than your ways
> and my thoughts than your thoughts.'
> ISAIAH 55:8–9

We would love access to a giant control panel for everything made. God in his wisdom has chosen the way of freedom and by and large lets tectonic plates shift, lava flow, locusts swarm, lions hunt. We should never forget all of it remains at his command, under his authority and always within his loving sight.

Bill McKibben writes in his book *The Comforting Whirlwind: God, Job and the scale of creation*:

> It is a buzzing, weird, stoic, abundant, reckless, haunting, painful, perfect planet. All of it matters, all of it is glorious. And all of it can speak to us in the deepest and most satisfying ways, if only we will let it.[13]

Over these next days together, we'll be listening to the voice of creation tell us about its creator. And we'll hear God speak of his great love for *all* he has made, a love that leaves nothing behind to hopeless destruction.

For reflection

When have you been confronted by your smallness and the vastness of all that surrounds you? How did it make you feel? In what ways is the mystery of God a comfort and in what ways is it challenging?

Prayer

Lord God, you are the father of the rain and the dew, the mother of ice and frost. You know the laws of the heavens and have dominion over the earth. I am in awe of you, and I bring you my worship now. Amen.

Huarango/algarrobo *Neltuma spp.*

One tree, two names! A Rocha in Peru has been planting native dry forest trees since 2009. Known as huarango in the south and algarrobo in the north, **Neltuma spp.** *trees are vital to the survival of dry forests, one of the most fragile ecosystems in the world.*

Day 13

Glimpses of glory

The heavens declare the glory of God;
    the skies proclaim the work of his hands.
Day after day they pour forth speech;
    night after night they reveal knowledge.
They have no speech, they use no words;
    no sound is heard from them.
Yet their voice goes out into all the earth,
    their words to the ends of the world.
In the heavens God has pitched a tent for the sun.
    It is like a bridegroom coming out of his chamber,
    like a champion rejoicing to run his course.
It rises at one end of the heavens
    and makes its circuit to the other;
    nothing is deprived of its warmth.

PSALM 19:1–6

The A Rocha International team recently took Gallup's CliftonStrengths quiz.[14] The idea is that instead of everyone trying to improve in areas of weakness, you identify your top strengths and those of your colleagues and focus on those. I was relieved, given my job title is director of communications, that my number one strength was communication. The description said that those with this strength like to hunt for the perfect phrase and are drawn towards dramatic words and powerful word combinations. This is very true of me. I got a lot of pleasure unpeeling the layers of the words and phrases in this psalm, and I hope you will too.

From the earliest times, the Hebrew Bible was copied by hand by scribes known as *soferim*. The literal translation of this word is 'counters'. Such was the importance placed on accuracy that a *sofer* could not make a single mistake in all the 304,805 letters on a scroll of the Torah. Each mark made by the ink was to communicate something of inexpressible worth and must be carried over identically from copy to copy. Just as much as writing, these scholars were counting, letter by letter.

The English word 'declare' in Psalm 19:1 is *mesaperim* in Hebrew, and it comes from the same root word as *sofarim*. The choice of this verb expresses that every single detail of creation has something to say about God. From the massive Goliath beetle with its gentle nature, to the okapi who can fully rotate their ears and catch noise from any direction, to the amazing glow-in-the-dark Casa Blanca lilies, all bear the fingerprints of their maker.

Creation is a book God himself has composed, and its meaning is clear and accessible to all who pay attention. More Hebrew: *maggid*, translated in the second line as 'proclaim', has overtones of expressing something in such an obvious way it can't be missed, an explanation with no subtlety at all. In the Jewish Passover seder, the Maggid is the part of the Exodus story that is told to the children present. The skies speak so clearly that absolutely all of us ought to catch what's being communicated.

What is it that these wordless voices speak out loudly enough to be heard from here to the ends of the earth? Paul spells it out in his letter to the early church in Rome:

> Since the creation of the world God's invisible qualities – his eternal power and divine nature – have been clearly seen, being understood from what has been made, so that people are without excuse.
> ROMANS 1:20

God is nothing if not a communicator. Jesus, who John calls 'the Word' in his gospel, told us in human language and in the action of his short earthly life what God is like. The Holy Spirit breathes clarity and understanding into our limited, closed minds. And the skies, crossed by the champion, the bridegroom sun who splashes his canvas with aubergine, apricot, sunflower, violet, crimson and azure, 'pour forth speech' (v. 2).

Thundering waterfalls and electric storms tell us of God's grandeur and terrifying power. Leaf veins and the richness in one speck of tulip pollen, the perfectly adapted skin of desert-dwelling snakes and the versatile design of an elephant's trunk, all say that God is a masterful designer, full of invention, creativity and playful ideas, mindful of the tiniest detail and always holding together the whole. What Jesus taught on hillsides and in homes, through miracles, friendships and in the opening of scripture, what he said about God's character and purposes on the cross, is echoed by creation, the works of his hands.

For reflection

Find somewhere you are able to see the sky. Ask God to help you listen to what it can tell you about him.

Prayer

Show me your glory in what you have made, holy God. Give me eyes that can see and ears alert to what is being said. Thank you for all the ways you express your nature, and that there is always more we can know. Amen.

Red-tailed hawk *Buteo jamaicensis*

Between 2005 and 2018, A Rocha Canada monitored the spring migration of hawks, eagles and other raptors in the Pembina Valley (Manitoba), an important migration corridor for birds of prey and other bird species.

Day 14

Sabbath for the land

'Speak to the Israelites and say to them: "When you enter the land I am going to give you, the land itself must observe a sabbath to the Lord. For six years sow your fields, and for six years prune your vineyards and gather their crops. But in the seventh year the land is to have a year of sabbath rest, a sabbath to the Lord. Do not sow your fields or prune your vineyards. Do not reap what grows of itself or harvest the grapes of your untended vines. The land is to have a year of rest. Whatever the land yields during the sabbath year will be food for you – for yourself, your male and female servants, and the hired worker and temporary resident who live among you, as well as for your livestock and the wild animals in your land. Whatever the land produces may be eaten"…

'You may ask, "What will we eat in the seventh year if we do not plant or harvest our crops?" I will send you such a blessing in the sixth year that the land will yield enough for three years. While you plant during the eighth year, you will eat from the old crop and will continue to eat from it until the harvest of the ninth year comes in.
    "'The land must not be sold permanently, because the land is mine and you reside in my land as foreigners and strangers.'"
LEVITICUS 25:2–7, 20–23

The early chapters of Genesis give us a foundational understanding of the relational logic which underpins the created order. All that is made is God's. God makes humankind in his image, and we are delegated to rule on his behalf. All of creation is a temple where God's presence dwells. The six days of making are followed by a day of rest, and this seven-day rhythm becomes not just a good suggestion for general well-being, but a vital part of the wiring, such that when it isn't followed things go badly wrong.

If you have had any Bible teaching, I'm confident you've heard the narrative arc of scripture explained in terms of four major movements: creation, fall, redemption, new creation. You may not have heard anything other than the human angle on the story, though. The fall was a disaster for people, and they then made it a disaster for everything else. No longer working in partnership with the land, they treated it like a slave. In turn, the land worked the human to death (Genesis 3:16–19). Thrown out of Eden, they lived in denial of their own nature and in conflict with the natural world. Redemption is for us people, and in our redemption is blessing for everything else. This part is present and ongoing. In God's reaching towards his people for reconciliation, his intention was for every part of creation to benefit. God's coming restoration of what is damaged, lost and defaced is not just a people-project: it is for all of creation.

Leviticus 25 sits at the point in Israel's history when they are about to end their desert wandering and enter a new Eden-like home. Rescued from the chaos of slavery, they have been formed as a free and well-ordered nation. These verses show clearly how God cares for this land where they will live. The rest that he himself undertook on the seventh day of creation, the sabbath he mandated in commandment number four of the famous ten, he intends that the land itself shall have. Each seventh year, the people of Israel are to be reminded that the land is the Lord's (v. 23) and not theirs; that it is the Lord who provides for their needs and that he can be trusted (v. 21); and that the land itself has a relationship with the Lord that is of more importance than the one they have (v. 4). For one year in seven, the land should rest and exist for God and for itself, not as a resource for us. In this way, the relational dynamic is held in health – as it was designed and intended. When things are done as the creator ordains, everything does well. And we all know the converse is true.

Not all of us are farmers, but we all live in a relationship of dependence on and power over land to some degree. Today's passage challenges us to remember that God cares deeply about the welfare of this land, and not just about us. He expects that as we are redeemed and restored, his image in us will lead us to be a blessing, not a curse, to the cosmos.

For reflection

Do I ever relate to land as anything other than a setting for my life and a source of resources to meet my needs? How can my understanding become more conformed to God's?

Prayer

Lord God, I am sorry that I have contributed to the stripping, depleting and overworking of the land. I am sorry I have not been part of giving your world the sabbath rest it needs. Thank you for your mercy and forgiveness. Bring health and healing to the soil, the water, the seeds and the creatures of this beautiful planet and let me play my part. Amen.

Long-tailed bat *Chalinolobus tuberculatus*

This endemic and rare species has been sighted on and around Mount Karioi through surveys and monitoring. The species holds the highest threat ranking of Nationally Critical in Aotearoa New Zealand.

Day 15

Impacted by the fall

The earth will be completely laid waste
   and totally plundered.
      The Lord has spoken this word.

The earth dries up and withers,
   the world languishes and withers,
   the heavens languish with the earth.
The earth is defiled by its people;
   they have disobeyed the laws,
violated the statutes
   and broken the everlasting covenant.
Therefore a curse consumes the earth;
   its people must bear their guilt.
Therefore earth's inhabitants are burned up,
   and very few are left.
The new wine dries up and the vine withers;
   all the merrymakers groan.

ISAIAH 24:3–7

When I was a student, one of my housemates had a video of a stand-up comedy set called *Glorious* (this was back in 1997, when we watched videos). She would take it like medicine for stress, boredom or minor ailments and after two years we all knew it word for word. One of my favourite parts was a routine about Noah's ark and the flood. It plays on the tension of animals, birds and creatures that move along the ground coming under God's judgement (Genesis 6:7). In what way, the comedian mused, are giraffes evil? Perhaps they eat more leaves than they should or hide berries so other giraffes starve to death. Dogs, he acknowledged, can be bad dogs for stealing biscuits. But they have every right to say to us people, 'Who are you to judge me? You human beings who've had genocide, war against people of different creeds, colours, religions, and I stole a biscuit?! Is that a crime?' And then there's the loophole that means swimming and floating things get off scot-free.[15]

The uncomfortable truth is that while humanity are the ones who fell from grace and continue to be extremely accomplished evil-doers, the consequences are felt by everything and everyone else. That comedian isn't the only one to look at the story of Noah's ark as one among many which paint the Old Testament God in an unflattering light, to say the least. It is bad enough that so many people were wiped out by the flood, but how could the drowning of a sweet, dewy-eyed and innocent baby donkey ever be justified? Animal welfare charities are the most popular in the UK by some distance – this is a hot-button issue for us Brits!

But while we might be outraged by photos of mangy abandoned pets and moved to throw some cash to the Battersea Dogs and Cats Home, we also slaughter one billion chickens each year, 95% of which are raised in battery farms in the most unimaginably cruel conditions. Dairy cattle are forced to overproduce milk, and intensively farmed pigs exhibit stress behaviours like biting their bars. We want cheap sausages, so you won't hear us piping up about that very much. Our intensive crop farming practices are designed to extract the maximum yield per acre, relying on the use of toxic chemicals, heavy water consumption, genetically modified seed and drastic reduction in areas of uncultivated, biodiversity-rich land. We produce more food than we need, which we either eat, causing all manner of obesity-related health issues, or throw out.

This prophecy of Isaiah draws clear lines between people breaking their covenant with God and a curse consuming the earth. It isn't God cursing the natural world; it is us. And it isn't a fairy story curse unleashed in a cloud of sparkling purple magic dust, but the uninterrupted sequence of cause and effect. The earth has been plundered by us. We have laid waste to it. We have defiled it (vv. 1, 5). Is it surprising that we now face a situation where more and more parts of the world are becoming uninhabitable due to extreme heat, desertification, devastating floods and hurricanes and the inability to grow food or access clean water?

The fall was caused by Adam and Eve's disobedience in choosing to break the only prohibition God had given them. This fractured their intimate relationship with God, and opened a crevasse through which sin entered the world. Human sin resulted immediately and dramatically in a broken relationship with the rest of creation. Our greed, selfishness and hatred have caused untold suffering to our non-human neighbours. The withering of the vine is not the result of some maniacal deity having a bad day. It is a good, loving, just God allowing his image-bearers their freedom.

For reflection

In what ways are we now bearing our guilt (v. 6) in misusing the planet? How does this hit close to home as well as further away?

Prayer

Lord, show me how to be a blessing to the earth, how to restore my relationship with your creation so that I am not a curse. Amen.

Grey-headed flying fox *Pteropus poliocephalus*

A Rocha Australia monitors several species, including the largest bat found in Australia, the grey-headed flying fox (listed as vulnerable).

Day 16

God's covenant with all life

'I now establish my covenant with you and with your descendants after you and with every living creature that was with you – the birds, the livestock and all the wild animals, all those that came out of the ark with you – every living creature on earth. I establish my covenant with you: never again will all life be destroyed by the waters of a flood; never again will there be a flood to destroy the earth.'

And God said, 'This is the sign of the covenant I am making between me and you and every living creature with you, a covenant for all generations to come: I have set my rainbow in the clouds, and it will be the sign of the covenant between me and the earth. Whenever I bring clouds over the earth and the rainbow appears in the clouds, I will remember my covenant between me and you and all living creatures of every kind. Never again will the waters become a flood to destroy all life. Whenever the rainbow appears in the clouds, I will see it and remember the everlasting covenant between God and all living creatures of every kind on the earth.'

So God said to Noah, 'This is the sign of the covenant I have established between me and all life on the earth.'

GENESIS 9:9–17

We are back with Noah, the flood and the ark today. The waters have receded, the passengers have disembarked and a new chapter for the world begins. This is the first biblical covenant recorded, and while it shares many elements of the covenants that follow it, there are two key differences.

In a biblical context, a covenant is a binding agreement between two or more parties, involving promises, responsibilities and blessings. There is often a sign which serves as a reminder of the commitment that has been made, and repercussions spelled out for breaking it. Here we see God initiating a covenant, a point I didn't want us to miss. We could easily take for granted the fact we have a God who time and again reaches towards us, making promises we don't deserve and haven't been asking for. There are a multitude of other religions formed around gods with no interest or kindly feelings towards the world. They have to be entreated, bribed with sacrifice and obedience, pestered and begged to pay attention. Yahweh, God Almighty, the Great I Am, extends invitation after invitation into faithful relationship with him.

This covenant is standard in having a sign – Abraham's sign was circumcision, the sabbath was the sign of Moses' covenant and David's was the coming Messiah. In Noah's covenant, the sign was a rainbow, which these days is used to represent a variety of other things instead. Hopefully it still serves as a reminder of God's faithfulness to those who believe, in the 21st century as it has for most of human history.

Now to the two ways this covenant is different to the others. The first is that only God has responsibilities. Humanity has no obligations upon which the fulfilment of God's promises is contingent. When we get to the covenants with Abraham, Moses and David, there are a whole lot of laws to be obeyed in order to reap the benefits and blessings. But in this covenant, whatever we do and however far we fall, 'never again will the waters become a flood to destroy all life' (v. 15).

A mere 40 days after humanity has become so vile he regretted making them, God is already assuring them that destruction on the scale they have just survived by the skin of their teeth is a one-off event.

The second is that this covenant is unique in being made not just between God and people, but between God and living creatures of all kinds – all life on earth in fact. We are all huddled together under the umbrella of God's protection and mercy. His care extends to birds and wild animals, as well as livestock, implying he isn't just interested in the creatures people have use for. This is his world and all of it matters to him in perpetuity – the covenant is 'everlasting' (v. 16).

The flood and the receding of the waters, cataclysmic as it must have been for those who experienced it first hand, was a faint reflection of the drama at creation, when God separated land from water. And while those who made it on to the ark must have felt it was the greatest rescue vessel ever made, it foreshadowed the salvation of any who want to be saved through simple faith in Jesus. And God in Jesus will keep his promise to grab the earth from the jaws of destruction and take it into its eternal destiny.

For reflection

How does the symbolism of the rainbow inspire us to embrace our responsibilities towards God's creation?

Prayer

Thank you, Lord, for your love and care for all living things. Thank you that you have always faithfully kept your promises, and we can trust you will keep this one. Amen.

Yellow-banded bumblebee *Bombus terricola*

We care for creation, no matter the size! The yellow-banded bumblebee, one of the earlier species to emerge in the spring, is listed under special concern in Canada.

Day 17

Jesus and creation

The Son is the image of the invisible God, the firstborn over all creation. For in him all things were created: things in heaven and on earth, visible and invisible, whether thrones or powers or rulers or authorities; all things have been created through him and for him. He is before all things, and in him all things hold together. And he is the head of the body, the church; he is the beginning and the firstborn from among the dead, so that in everything he might have the supremacy. For God was pleased to have all his fullness dwell in him, and through him to reconcile to himself all things, whether things on earth or things in heaven, by making peace through his blood, shed on the cross.
COLOSSIANS 1:15–20

I have been around conversations and debates about the connection between nature conservation and Christianity since I was five years old, when my parents founded A Rocha.

I am aware, therefore, that there are those who believe there *isn't* a connection; that God only cares about humans and therefore, depending on what this care for humans looks like, we as his followers should only be concerned with saving souls and/or with human well-being. In a conversation I was having with a group of people recently, one said, 'Of course, the only reason the state of the world matters is because people and particularly the poor rely on it.' Everyone other than me nodded and made agreeing noises. I said, thereby creating an awkward moment for us all, 'Doesn't it matter because it matters to God?'

As individual humans we all place ourselves at the centre of the universe. We are the protagonist in the drama, the number one to be looked out for by ourselves and ideally by everyone else too. We do that as a species too. Think about the word 'environment'. It has its etymological roots in the Old French *environ*, meaning surround or enclose. There is us, and then everything else: our surroundings. We look at a lake and see water we can use to drink, wash and farm with, in which there are fish we can eat, and around which there are rocks we can build with. It is all so useful and we use it greedily until it is too polluted or depleted to serve our needs any longer. The soil, the air, the vegetation and the living creatures on land and in sea – these are resources, there for us.

These verses from Colossians take our telescopes and turn them around. We have been looking through the wrong end and thus our perspective has been all wrong. All things have been created by Jesus, and – the bit we often miss entirely – for Jesus. The waterfalls, the panda bears, the tulips, the hummingbirds, the sun and the moon: we enjoy these things. They bless us. Some of them literally keep us alive. But that's not their point. They exist for Jesus. He is the originator, the first, the best and the purpose of all of it.

As a man, Jesus was fully part of creation. He walked on the earth and ate of its fruit; he was drenched by the rain and warmed by the sun; he rode on a young donkey, watched the birds and knew the beauty of the wildflowers. He withdrew in nature to meet with his Father and knew the harshness of the wilderness. As God, Jesus also had authority over creation, turning water into wine, stilling a raging storm. Is it any wonder that at the moment of his death there was a total solar eclipse and an earthquake?

And as creator of all, is it any wonder that his resurrection has implications for everything? Through his blood, *all things* find reconciliation and peace with God (v. 20).

For reflection

What difference would it make to how we live in the world if we really understood that all of it is for Jesus?

Prayer

Use the verses in today's reading as a basis for prayer and worship.

Barn owl *Tyto alba*

A Rocha prioritises monitoring species to help us understand a place and the relationships at play within it.

Day 18

Promised redemption

> I consider that our present sufferings are not worth comparing with the glory that will be revealed in us. For the creation waits in eager expectation for the children of God to be revealed. For the creation was subjected to frustration, not by its own choice, but by the will of the one who subjected it, in hope that the creation itself will be liberated from its bondage to decay and brought into the freedom and glory of the children of God.
> We know that the whole creation has been groaning as in the pains of childbirth right up to the present time. Not only so, but we ourselves, who have the firstfruits of the Spirit, groan inwardly as we wait eagerly for our adoption to sonship, the redemption of our bodies. For in this hope we were saved. But hope that is seen is no hope at all. Who hopes for what they already have? But if we hope for what we do not yet have, we wait for it patiently.
> ROMANS 8:18–25

For as long as conservation has been a thing, conservationists have debated the relationship between humans and nature. For some, humans are a cancer, bringing death and destruction to species and habitats, every part of which has intrinsic value and the right to exist and flourish. People are the ones subjecting creation to frustration (v. 20) and the most effective tool of conservation is the establishment of protected areas – that is, areas protected from us.

They have a point. WWF's *Living Planet Report 2022* revealed global wildlife populations had fallen by an average of 69% since 1970.[16]

The drivers of biodiversity loss in general are all down to us: changing land and water use, overconsumption and exploitation, pollution, climate change and invasive species. As the Egyptians were cruel masters over the Israelite slaves, so arguably have we been over the rest of creation – just ask a battery chicken.

If the 'humans as cancer' attitude sits at one end of a spectrum, at the other is the idea that the goal of conservation is to preserve nature purely and simply for its role in our well-being. We need nature to do well so we can continue to use it. The environmental catastrophe unfolding before our eyes is already impacting us severely and particularly the poor and vulnerable. Therein lies the value of nature and our imperative to guard and restore it.

The biblical world view is radically different to both those perspectives. Here in Romans 8, Paul pictures a creation waiting with impatient longing for 'the children of God to be revealed', for a time when we live the same resurrected lives as the Easter Jesus, entering fully into our intended identities as God's image-bearers. God's design was for humans to rule on his behalf, in the manner he rules, such that we bless, protect, guide, nurture, love and care for this world and all who live here. People and nature belong together, are made for interdependence, are created for harmony and wholeness. We have all suffered the consequences of sin, and we are all waiting to be brought into freedom from decay.

Two realities then: the reality of 'our present sufferings' and the reality of the 'freedom and glory' for which we wait. What is the bridge from one to the other? As always there are a variety of theories on this, ranging from the apocalyptic wipe-out of Prototype 1 to be replaced with a new and better version, to the assumption that we must make do and mend what we have because, in the words of a Christian conservationist I recently met: 'There is no big daddy coming to save us. This world is all we have, and God only works through human hands.' Here in Romans 8, Paul uses the language of childbirth and, in so doing, beautifully illustrates how continuity and discontinuity coexist in what we await. There will be a moment of violent and disruptive change from one order to the next; as a newborn baby becomes separated from the mother's body, so this age in this universe will make way for the next age.

Since I was last pregnant, technology has evolved to the point where a scan can show you a pretty clear picture of your unborn child. During the final trimester, they don't look all that different to the infant you will, all going well, hold in your arms before too long. As the baby inside is the same baby outside, so will the creation be recognisable – restored and renewed, not razed and rebuilt. In these verses, N.T. Wright says, what Paul 'has in mind is not the unmaking of creation or simply its steady development but the drastic and dramatic birth of the new creation from the womb of the old'.[17]

There isn't a lot of good news when it comes to the state of the planet and our immediate, let alone long-term, outlook. This was not the case when Paul wrote his letter to the Christians in Rome, though they had their own suffering and just as much need for hope. Like the early church, we were 'saved in this hope', the hope of the redemption of our bodies (vv. 23–24). And with us, the whole of creation will be restored to life and health – not by us and our efforts, but by the power, grace and love of its Maker and Saviour.

For reflection

Where have you seen or experienced creation's 'bondage to decay'? Have you heard any groaning, and if so, how did you respond?

Prayer

Lord, our present sufferings and those of the whole creation are acute. We know we are culpable for much of this. Please forgive us and in your mercy hold back the devastating consequences of how we have used and abused this world of yours. Thank you for giving us the hope of redemption. Thank you that your plans for good encompass all you have made. Help us wait patiently and live righteously until you come again. Amen.

Northern red-legged frog *Rana aurora*

Since 2009, A Rocha Canada has inventoried annual egg mass surveys for pond-breeding amphibians like this 'special concern' frog throughout the Little Campbell River watershed (British Columbia).

Day 19

Earthly hope

After the Sabbath, at dawn on the first day of the week, Mary Magdalene and the other Mary went to look at the tomb.
There was a violent earthquake, for an angel of the Lord came down from heaven and, going to the tomb, rolled back the stone and sat on it. His appearance was like lightning, and his clothes were white as snow. The guards were so afraid of him that they shook and became like dead men.
The angel said to the women, 'Do not be afraid, for I know that you are looking for Jesus, who was crucified. He is not here; he has risen, just as he said. Come and see the place where he lay. Then go quickly and tell his disciples: "He has risen from the dead and is going ahead of you into Galilee. There you will see him." Now I have told you.'
So the women hurried away from the tomb, afraid yet filled with joy, and ran to tell his disciples. Suddenly Jesus met them. 'Greetings,' he said. They came to him, clasped his feet and worshipped him.
MATTHEW 28:1–9

In the way that you can get glasses that only allow certain wavelengths through, many people read the resurrection accounts and only see its human impact, and impact on our lives post-death. Let's read this text from Matthew's gospel without filtering lenses and see what is there for all of creation and for the present, not the distant future.

With those glasses off, we can see what is staring us in the face: Jesus was resurrected in *this world*. One of the windows that has let the most light and fresh air into my faith is 'The Chronicles of Narnia' by

C.S. Lewis. In *The Lion, the Witch and the Wardrobe*, four children stumble through the back of a cupboard into a snowy landscape, which has some similarities to where they came from but turns out to be a parallel universe running on different time, with its own story of creation, fall and redemption, and animals who speak the same language as humans. The lion Aslan, the Christ figure, is slain on the Stone Table at the hands of the White Witch in place of the traitor Edmund to settle an ancient score. His resurrection instigates a great thaw, the long winter finally making way for spring. The children eventually leave Narnia. But we live in the world to which our Saviour returned from death. In the dark of predawn, under the stars and the moon of this very solar system, Jesus walked free from the captivity of death, alive and breathing in great lungfuls of Judean air. He would soon share food with his friends. He had feet that could be clasped.

In her assumption that he was the gardener (John 20:15), Mary was not entirely wrong. All that is and lives and grows is spoken into being and sustained by Jesus. His is the image we were designed to reflect in the way we tend this garden-globe. His bodily resurrection is resounding reaffirmation of the goodness of creation, if we needed it, and it renews our Genesis mandate.

Ruling in his stead means involving ourselves in earthly tasks, sticking our hands deep into the soil, as his kingdom comes 'on earth as it is in heaven' (Matthew 6:10). It is why A Rocha understands our work of nature conservation as worship before anything else. When we clear a dry meadow in Switzerland of invasive shrubs, when we protect fluffy ōi chicks from predators in New Zealand, when we take the Ghanaian government to court to prevent it handing out mining licences that would destroy Atewa forest, or when we give children wondrous adventures in the wild outdoors in Canada so they experience the wonder and beauty of nature, we are honouring the one who made it and loves it.

Jesus' resurrection had direct and immediate effect on creation. On a small scale, there was an earthquake as an angel rolled away the enormous stone blocking the tomb. On a cosmic scale, a new era was inaugurated. Yesterday we considered the mysterious tension between the biblical vision of both continuity and discontinuity. This creation has a long-term future, but at the same time, there's an epic shake-up and remaking to come. While we may not understand how things might unfold at the close-detail level, we can be confident that our 'labour in the Lord is not in vain' (1 Corinthians 15:58).

For reflection

Put yourselves in the story from the perspective of the Marys as they suddenly come across Jesus, who they had so recently witnessed be put to death. Picture the ground, damp with the morning dew, feel the cool early air on your face and the light of the sunrise reflecting from Jesus' face. He is in this place with you. He is in this world.

Prayer

Holy God, you made this world good and you loved it such that you became part of it and returned to it in resurrected life. Help me not to miss the significance of what you did for the whole creation. Help me not to miss the hope you have given us for now, not just for the future. Amen.

Grey-faced petrel/ōi *Pterodroma gouldi*

A Rocha has been working with the community since 2009 to re-establish Mount Karioi, New Zealand, for seabirds like the ōi. More than 47 ōi chicks have fledged over the last six years!

Day 20

Heaven is coming here

Then I saw 'a new heaven and a new earth,' for the first heaven and the first earth had passed away, and there was no longer any sea. I saw the Holy City, the new Jerusalem, coming down out of heaven from God, prepared as a bride beautifully dressed for her husband. And I heard a loud voice from the throne saying, 'Look! God's dwelling-place is now among the people, and he will dwell with them. They will be his people, and God himself will be with them and be their God.
REVELATION 21:1–3

The other day I had to get a very early train. We pulled out of the station in pitch darkness and after about 20 minutes with my head down over my laptop, I looked up to see the sky daubed in outrageous fluorescent magenta, pearlescent peach, silvery blue and deep, velvety purple. I wanted to stand on my seat, wave and point and make sure the whole carriage had the chance to see it. I restrained myself and only pointed it out to those in my immediate vicinity, who were appropriately grateful, I'm glad to report. It was extraordinarily beautiful, and exactly the kind of sky from which the new Jerusalem might descend.

A younger me might have looked at the same sky and instead wondered if heaven would be a bit like that – a giant, glowing, abstract painting through which souls would float for eternity. If anything other than our souls survived judgement day, young me might have thought, it'll be the colour pink. But here in Revelation we have the marriage of heaven and earth and God making his home among us.

This is not a rescue of human souls from creation but the healing and restoration of all things. As God never intended to rescue Israel from the Gentiles but to rescue them so they would lead the Gentiles to him, so humans are rescued to become the blessing to all creation he intended us to be.

The idea of heaven as a place we go when we die is deeply entrenched. But the Bible doesn't say anything about anyone going to anywhere in the afterlife.[18] That's something we made up by ourselves. From Genesis to Revelation and everywhere in between, God's long-term love commitment to his entire creation is writ large. From the Sokoke scops owl to the mangabey monkey, from the bee orchid to the Salish sucker, each part of this world adds its voice to a choir that rejoices God's heart. As the temple curtain separating sinners from the altar was torn at the moment Jesus took his last breath on the cross, so will his second coming shred the veil hiding God's realm. The dual realities will unite: the end of our long separation.

If you are someone blessed with access to a bit of unspoilt nature, none of this will surprise you. It is a common experience to be standing at the top of a mountain or under a waterfall or beneath a forest canopy and to sense God's proximity. Watching the sunrise from my train, I wondered how anyone could see a sky like that and not be compelled to worship the artist, but the truth is I could well have been the only Christian on all seven crowded carriages. But one day, 'The earth will be filled with the knowledge of the glory of the Lord as the waters cover the sea' (Habakkuk 2:14). This is the future, and it is glorious for us and glorious for the rest of creation.

For reflection

Where in nature do you feel most aware of the presence and glory of God? What glimpses have you had of what the new heavens and new earth might be like?

Prayer

Heavenly Father, sometimes I miss the goodness of the world you have made because I'm not looking; I'm absorbed in my troubles and my busyness. But when I pay attention, all around me your glory is evident. Thank you that in the life to come there will be more beauty, more diversity, more colours and smells and textures and noises, not less. Come, Lord Jesus! Bring heaven to earth. Amen.

European hedgehog *Erinaceus europaeus*

There are 200,000–250,000 hedgehogs in the UK, down from 30 million in 1950. The hedgehog is included in A Rocha UK's Target 25 initiative, which focuses on managing sites to increase populations of 25 declining species, species groups and habitats.

III

People and people

In the quiet of the morning,
in the whispers of the night,
I feel your presence near me,
in your arms, I find delight.
Every heartbeat, every moment,
you're the one who knows my soul,
in your love, I am certain,
with you, I am whole.

WHAT YOU'VE JUST READ is verse one of an AI-generated song produced by ChatGPT in response to my request for contemporary worship lyrics. This does not make a definitive statement about the framing of religious experience in the 21st century, but I found it interesting nonetheless. The robot has written something perfectly suited for a hyper-individualistic culture, in which each person seeks personal, intimate experiences with God which provide them with various kinds of emotional gratification.

The songbook of the Psalms has plenty of lyrics expressing one person's thoughts and feelings towards God. Psalm 139 is a beautiful celebration of every human life's worth and visibility to the Father of all. But most of the Psalms, indeed most of the Bible, assumes worship to be a communal activity. Much of the work and wonder of the spiritual life happens within relationship.

Genesis describes Adam as alone in the garden before Eve's creation – no matter that he had God's company. The fall devastated the humans' relationship with God, but also caused problems between them. On the night before his death, Jesus prayed at length for love and unity between those who would follow him in times to come. Yes, he cares for me. He also cares for *us*. Together we are his body on earth. Together we are the temple where he dwells. Together we demonstrate the power of his risen life to transform the world.

Day 21

A brotherhood of man

> Then the Lord said to Cain, 'Why are you angry? Why is your face downcast? If you do what is right, will you not be accepted? But if you do not do what is right, sin is crouching at your door; it desires to have you, but you must rule over it.'
> Now Cain said to his brother Abel, 'Let's go out to the field.' While they were in the field, Cain attacked his brother Abel and killed him.
> Then the Lord said to Cain, 'Where is your brother Abel?'
> 'I don't know,' he replied. 'Am I my brother's keeper?'
> The Lord said, 'What have you done? Listen! Your brother's blood cries out to me from the ground.
> GENESIS 4:6–10

We've started in medias res, a scene taut with dangerous energy from the first line of dialogue. A flashback would show Cain sweating under the sun to bring in his crops, pulling a sheaf of grain from the heap for the altar only to find that instead of responding in gratitude, God's favour is withheld, and worse, lavished on his younger brother for his offering of lamb fat. Fast growing seeds of jealousy and resentment are sown, and he will soon reap destruction.

The text doesn't tell us why the fruits of the soil were less acceptable than the sheep fat. People have speculated that it had to do with the respective givers' motivation and attitude in giving, the quality of the gift, perhaps the degree to which they might have observed any guidance they'd received. Whatever the reason, Cain feels rejected, initially gets angry with God, and then turns on his brother. A fractured relationship with God turns things ugly between us humans. This may have been the first blood shed, but rivers have been spilt in violent malice since then. If you are tempted to point out at this juncture that you have never stabbed anyone, may I gently direct you to 1 John 3:15: 'Anyone who hates a brother or sister is a murderer.'

This is a spool that has been unravelling since the beginning. If we trace back to where things began to go wrong, there are signs that a murder would happen sooner or later. The details in Genesis 1—3 are nothing if not portentous. But in all three chapters, there are also signs of hope and evidence of God's gritty faithfulness. We'll look at both the brokenness and healing balm held out to us.

Back in the garden of Eden, God warned Adam and Eve that if they ate the fruit of a particular tree they would die. The serpent says they won't die, they'll just know good and evil. Of course, the pernicious lie had an element of truth, but it masked the heart of the matter. Spiritual death is far deadlier and lasts forever, and the fruit would have the exact effect God said it would have in that regard. Cain's decision to kill his brother takes him into a living death of banishment from the Lord's presence. Abel's blood still calls to his heavenly Father.

For some reason, Eve chooses to believe the word of a serpent over God's, along with a couple of her own reasons (seems like it would be tasty, and it is super aesthetically pleasing. You know what? I'm going to treat myself!) A generation down the line, and God spells out once more the choice to do what is right or be defeated by sin. Notice: God remains in relationship with humankind. We're not told how, but his voice communicates to Cain with complete clarity. He may not be around for peaceful strolls in the cool of the day, but he has not abandoned them – far from it.

So Eve, Adam and all who came after them knew good and evil, but the fall did not take away the ability to resist evil. Bad decisions are not inevitable. Sin may be at the door, but 'you must rule over it' (v. 7). That implies you *can* rule over it. Our freedom is frightening and often misused, and it is also a great gift. It leaves us with the ability to listen to God and obey and grow ever closer until one day, in the new heavens and earth, there will be no distance between us at all.

Back to Cain. He made a calculated decision, and there is no doubt at all his crime was premeditated. This is murder, not manslaughter; no red mist descended, overriding rationality. Cain invited his brother out to a field calmly enough that Abel went along without coercion, presumably to make sure there were no witnesses to the attack. Just as his parents had hidden from God, so Cain is fool enough to believe he can keep what he's done a secret. Given the opportunity to come clean, he lies with an audaciously cheeky boldness along the lines of 'How should I know? I'm not his babysitter!' Adam and Eve before him were also given the chance to be accountable for their actions, but as you'll remember, the man blames the woman and the woman blames the serpent.

This is a terrible story in so many ways. It is also horribly familiar because such things keep happening: as the Scottish poet Robert Burns put it, 'Man's inhumanity to man, Makes countless thousands mourn.' Sin means we hurt each other dreadfully. But let's end on a brighter note. The restoration of our relationship with God through Jesus gives us every hope we can do better between ourselves.

For reflection

Prayerfully bring to mind someone you struggle to love. Maybe they have hurt you badly or perhaps you just find them intensely irritating. Ask God to help you see them with his eyes. What might the Holy Spirit want to reveal to you about choices you could make in this relationship?

Prayer

Heavenly Father, I know that my sin puts strain on my relationships. Sometimes my jealousy, anger, hurt and desire for power make me hateful. Please forgive me and help me be someone who brings peace. Amen.

Norfolk hawker *Aeshna isoceles*

This dragonfly is one of many found at Foxearth Meadows, A Rocha UK's reserve dedicated to dragonflies and damselflies in Essex.

Day 22

Forgive, forgive, forgive, repeat

> Then Peter came to Jesus and asked, 'Lord, how many times shall I forgive my brother or sister who sins against me? Up to seven times?'
>
> Jesus answered, 'I tell you, not seven times, but seventy-seven times.
>
> 'Therefore, the kingdom of heaven is like a king who wanted to settle accounts with his servants...
>
> 'Then the master called the servant in. "You wicked servant," he said, "I cancelled all that debt of yours because you begged me to. Shouldn't you have had mercy on your fellow servant just as I had on you?" In anger his master handed him over to the jailers to be tortured, until he should pay back all he owed.
>
> 'This is how my heavenly Father will treat each of you unless you forgive your brother or sister from your heart.'
>
> MATTHEW 18:21–23, 32–35

You may have noticed today's reading was missing a section. Please do find and read it in your Bible if you have one – I only cut it for length. In summary, the wicked servant had been forgiven an impossible debt of ten thousand bags of gold, only to viciously assault and have imprisoned a fellow servant who owed him the pitiful amount of a hundred silver coins. It would also be worthwhile going to the start of the chapter for context. This conversation and parable come after a set of teachings dealing with painful issues that often come up among believers. They'd already discussed humility, how seriously bad it is to cause a brother or sister in Christ to struggle in the life of faith and how to handle conflict. All this acknowledges the reality that even passionate Christians don't always get along. There's a pragmatism to biblical guidance on behaviour, ethics and attitudes at the same time as an uncompromising call to 'be perfect... as your heavenly Father is perfect' (Matthew 5:48).

Jesus was a master storyteller, and to get the most from his teaching we need to become master story hearers. We need to attune ourselves to the beating heart in the body of detail, listening as attentively as a surgeon with a stethoscope. If we deduce from this interaction between Jesus and Peter that there is a limit (77) to the number of times we have to forgive a particular person, or that if we don't our heavenly Father will torture us, we have misheard.

The heart of this story is that we have been forgiven an unpayable debt by God, through Jesus, and in the light of that fact, we are not at liberty to withhold forgiveness when we are wronged. Citizens of the kingdom of heaven are required to forgive one another. Forgiving a repeat offender three times was considered generous in the Jewish tradition of Peter's time. Many today would consider it beyond generous and heading towards absurdity. So what Peter was suggesting must have felt an extravagant stretch, while retaining a sensible limit. In saying 'not seven, but seventy-seven times' Jesus was effectively removing all limits: forgive until you lose count. He was changing the paradigm entirely. He was changing it because in the terms of his story, he is the king who has mercy on those who ask to have their impossible-to-set-right wrongs written off, and we are those who, having been 'made right in God's sight by the blood of Christ' (Romans 5:9, NLT), have no grounds to offer any less.

I recently caught up with a dear friend, who I'll call Martha. We'd not seen each other for six years, as we live on different continents, and we had a lot of ground to cover. Early on in our day together, I mentioned her church, which I knew was a big and happy part of her life, and she made the kind of throwaway comment which my long antenna registered as hinting at something complicated. With the sun going down over the lake, we wrapped up in blankets, made tea and returned to the matter of church. Just prior to the Covid pandemic, Martha's church, where she'd been for over 20 years – serving on the leadership team, known, loved and respected – disbanded. She was sad but had some excitement at the prospect of finding a new church community.

At the first church she joined she was met with an odd hostility. Eventually, she heard why. A woman who had heard her speak at a conference had later had a 'prophetic dream' revealing Martha to be a Satanist and had taken it upon herself to take this revelation to the leadership of the church once she heard Martha was there. Confounded and dismayed, she decided to move on.

The rumours had reached the next church before her. This time, she figured she'd stick it out and over time show she was absolutely not a Satanist, but rather someone who lived wholeheartedly for Jesus. Week in, week out she was treated with suspicion and unkindness, blocked from any kind of role, and avoided by the leadership. My eyes were on stalks when she told me she had tolerated this situation for an entire year! And they welled up as she talked about her commitment to forgiving the dreamer and those in the two churches who had treated her so appallingly. I was holding on to a grudge for a far lesser wrong and in Martha's total freedom from bitterness and lack of any desire for retribution, I saw I had much further to go in my own road to forgiveness.

Martha didn't stay around to be abused forever. She shook the dust from her feet and moved on. Forgiveness does not mean putting ourselves in reach of harm. It does not mean forgetting what has happened to us. It does not mean continuing in relationship with the person who has hurt us. It does not mean we want them to escape justice, punishment or consequences.

In Jesus' story, the debt of ten thousand bags of gold could only be settled by the sale of the servant, his wife and their children and everything they owned. The king had the right to demand this, but instead he 'took pity on him, cancelled the debt and let him go' (v. 27). God has taken pity on us. Forgiveness means we, in the same way, take pity and release the one who has wronged us to be judged by God (and if appropriate, the legal system). By the power of the Holy Spirit, we can forgive.

For reflection

What are your ten thousand bags of gold? And who owes you some silver coins?

Prayer

Merciful God, you have forgiven me so much – more than I know, and more than I can face. Thank you. I struggle to extend the same grace when I am betrayed, wounded and mistreated. I want to see others suffer as I have, or worse, if I'm being honest. But you ask me to forgive as I have been forgiven. Please give me your strength to do this. In the name of Jesus. Amen.

Ocellated lizard *Timon lepidus*

A Rocha France is studying the ocellated lizard, a species endemic to southwestern Europe, to determine the population and distribution at both French study sites (Vallée des Baux and Domaine des Courmettes).

Day 23

Costly love

'As the Father has loved me, so have I loved you. Now remain in my love. If you keep my commands, you will remain in my love, just as I have kept my Father's commands and remain in his love. I have told you this so that my joy may be in you and that your joy may be complete. My command is this: love each other as I have loved you. Greater love has no one than this: to lay down one's life for one's friends. You are my friends if you do what I command. I no longer call you servants, because a servant does not know his master's business. Instead, I have called you friends, for everything that I learned from my Father I have made known to you. You did not choose me, but I chose you and appointed you so that you might go and bear fruit – fruit that will last – and so that whatever you ask in my name the Father will give you. This is my command: love each other.'
JOHN 15:9–17

One of my guilty viewing pleasures is a Netflix show called *Love is Blind*. A pool of singles get to know the opposite sex in pods that keep them from seeing each other. Over the course of a couple of weeks, they form attachments and begin to date (if you can call talking to a stranger through a wall dating). Some couples then become exclusive, and then a handful get engaged – after which they meet and see what the other person looks like for the first time. The premise of the show is that true love has little to do with physical attraction. This theory is tested as the engaged couples head off for a romantic location for a holiday, return to their home towns to cohabit and meet each other's family and friends, and finally head down the aisle where – cliff-hanger! – they may or may not say 'I do.'

One of the couples who took the plunge in season 3, Alexa and Brennon, exchanged these vows. Brennon said, 'I pledge to you my love, everything that I am. Our love is never-ending, and we will remain forevermore in our marriage, even during football season. Before our friends, family and the world, I pledge my love and my life to you, in sickness and in health, for richer, for poorer.'

Alexa then responded with her vows, saying, 'Never in a million years did I think that I would find the love of my life on the other side of a pod wall. You make me laugh, you make me think and, more than anything else, you make me happy. I can't wait to build the rest of our futures together.'

I find this whole scenario an interesting counterpoint to how Jesus speaks about love in today's reading. These two may arguably have transcended lust by committing to one another 'sight unseen', to use the show's catchphrase, but Brennon's idea of sacrificial fidelity is to stay married during football season and Alexa's vows are based on how Brennan makes her feel. To their credit, at the time of writing they remain happily wed, but when Jesus says the word love (nine times in eight verses), he's talking about something very different, and not just because he's not addressing married love.

Jesus says love is the laying down of your life – which, plot spoiler, he's about to go on to do quite literally. And then he says we should love each other as he has loved us. Gulp. What could this mean?

There are many Greek words which translators have no option but to capture in our one English word love. Jesus was using *agape* here. This was known as the highest form of love, the love from God to people and their reciprocal love of God. *Agape* is self-giving, sacrificial and persistent. As babies learn to smile from the smiling faces beaming into theirs, so we learn *agape* as we receive and remain in the love of Jesus.

At first glance, remaining in the love of Jesus might sound a bit like basking in a sauna of comforting, pink emotion. It is a lot grittier, though, and in these verses is defined as keeping his commands (vv. 10, 14). One of his commands is set out with sparkling clarity right here. Twice – in verses 12 and 17: 'This is my command: love each other.'

In his death and resurrection, Jesus took our small, floppy idea of love and blew it up like the world's biggest ever balloon. He *commands* that we love one another in the same way that he is loved by his Father, and he loves us. The Easter story puts us on a different footing as a community of believers. We are not bound together by pleasant feelings or common interests, but by a love that leads us to lay ourselves down for one another.

I find this challenging, terrifying and daunting, but I want more than anything to be a friend of Jesus, so I have no choice but to press on in my (pathetic) efforts to love as he defines it. How about you?

For reflection

Did you catch the reference to joy in verse 11? When have you found joy in obedience to Christ in this area of love for others?

Prayer

Father, your love is unwavering, generous, unrestrained and costly. Thank you for loving me. Help me love my brothers and sisters in faith in the way you command. Give me strength, because I can't do it on my own. Amen.

Atewa slippery frog *Conraua sagyimase*

A new species to science was discovered in Atewa Forest in 2006: the Atewa slippery frog. A Rocha is working with the Forestry Research Institute of Ghana to survey Atewa's streams for the frog, using passive sound recorders to record their nocturnal calls.

Day 24

Banking on each other

> All the believers were one in heart and mind. No one claimed that any of their possessions was their own, but they shared everything they had. With great power the apostles continued to testify to the resurrection of the Lord Jesus. And God's grace was so powerfully at work in them all that there was no needy person among them. For from time to time those who owned land or houses sold them, brought the money from the sales and put it at the apostles' feet, and it was distributed to anyone who had need.
> ACTS 4:32–35

All the believers were one in heart and mind. They shared all their opinions and felt fondly about each other, especially on weekdays when there was no home group. Sometimes if the worship song was particularly moving, they'd hold hands and eye-contact in a circle. God's grace was so powerfully at work in them all that sometimes prayer meetings went on a bit longer than planned. From time to time, those who had houses with big gardens would invite church members over for a bring-and-share picnic. Leftovers would be distributed to anyone with space in their fridge.

As you'll know, having just read the actual description of the early church, the above is a tongue-in-cheek distortion. But it perhaps reflects today's understanding of what it means to be 'one in heart and mind' – matters of emotion (heart) and intellect (mind). In the world of Acts, it meant, among other things, no longer seeing possessions as one's own and using individual resources for the benefit of the community. One impact of the resurrection on the believers was a transformation of their relationship to their finances. We might argue that theirs was a society without a social security safety net, so communities were relied on more heavily to provide for the vulnerable than we are today, in the global north. We could say that the early church was small and idealistic and not a realistic model for 21st-century Christians. We may want to believe that there aren't acutely needy people in our churches.

Jesus said, 'Where your treasure is, there your heart will be also' (Matthew 6:21) and 'You cannot serve both God and Money' (Matthew 6:24). He came with an invitation to belong to a kingdom with a ruler who asks us to give him everything and who then sets us free and gives us riches that 'moths and vermin do not destroy' (Matthew 6:20). Citizens of this kingdom become family and share both burdens and joys. Our finances come under God's authority and become a conduit of his grace.

I'm not describing the unattainable ideals of utopia, but how the life of the church can and often does work. I have an enormous number of personal stories to draw from. Here are just a handful, to which I know you'll be able to add your own. When I was a child and living in Portugal, my dad needed major surgery at short notice. The church we'd belonged to before we moved abroad housed and fed our family of six for several months until Dad was well enough for us to go home. When I got engaged, I was happy and then somewhat worried, as we had not a bean to put towards a wedding. In the event, every detail of the day was a gift – culminating in the moment we asked for an invoice for the church hall where we'd had the reception and were told it had been settled. When Shawn and I had our first baby, we had no money for a car seat, buggy, baby monitor and all that jazz. Our church kitted us out in style. I was even taken shopping for maternity clothes. When we had an emergency in South Africa, our church family gave money to cover my flight and other expenses.

In turn, when we have had financial breathing room, we have experienced the delight of being someone else's answer to prayer. Funnily enough, the Bible was right that 'it is more blessed to give than to receive' (Acts 20:35)!

The Christian life connects us in real and practical ways to other Christians. This includes a responsibility to meet one another's material needs, according to our ability. When we do this, it increases the power of our witness, just as it did in the early church. Jesus said the world would know who his disciples were because of how they loved each other (John 13). Let's say we love each other and then put our money where our mouth is.

For reflection

What are your most valuable possessions? Do you consider them your own? How could they be used generously and creatively to bless someone in need in your church?

Prayer

Provider God, everything I have is yours. Show me where there is need and give me the willingness to share. Your kingdom come, your will be done on earth as in heaven. Amen.

Southern festoon *Zerynthia polyxena*

This butterfly is on the threatened species list in France – it depends on one unique plant and a specific habitat. The team in the Vallée des Baux (near Arles) has been managing its habitat and studying its population for over a decade.

Day 25

One for all and all for one

'My prayer is not for them alone. I pray also for those who will believe in me through their message, that all of them may be one, Father, just as you are in me and I am in you. May they also be in us so that the world may believe that you have sent me. I have given them the glory that you gave me, that they may be one as we are one – I in them and you in me – so that they may be brought to complete unity. Then the world will know that you sent me and have loved them even as you have loved me.
JOHN 17:20–23

My daughter and I were on the bus coming home from a trip to town when she got her phone out and started messaging. She's a teenager – that's not unusual behaviour. But then my phone buzzed; she was messaging me.

> *Her:* We are literally watching this girl's relationship fall apart on the phone. It's so sad.
> *Me (realising she's been eavesdropping too):* I know!! He was gay?
> *Her:* Think so. Massive plot twist.
> *Me:* Doesn't want his fam to know.
> *Her:* This is more interesting than anything I have heard in a long time. I can't hear!!!
> *Me:* Need to do lip reading.
> *Her:* U can't stare at her. She'll know that we're listening.
> *Me:* But I need to.
> *Her:* No Mum. You can't. Stay strong.

Eavesdropping on public transport is one of my favourite things and apparently my offspring enjoys it too! We can be glad that John was also an eavesdropper, because thanks to that we get to listen in to a conversation between Jesus and his heavenly Father. As it happens, they are talking about us! We are those who believe in him through the message of his first followers and friends (v. 20), those with him that night, the night of his last Passover meal. There are many things he could have prayed about. What he expresses are two clear desires for us, which both achieve the same thing.

The first desire is that we 'may be one, Father, just as you are in me and I am in you… one as we are one' (vv. 21–22). Jesus prays for complete unity among believers, mirroring the unity of the Trinity, three persons and a single God.

The second desire he has is that we 'also be in us' (v. 21). The phrases 'in Christ', 'in the Lord' and 'in him' can be found 164 times in the letters of Paul alone. Being in Christ doesn't mean being inside him, like a person in a coat, a letter in an envelope or a cow in a field. John Stott said it was 'to be organically united to Christ, as a limb is in the body or a branch is in the tree. It is this personal relationship with Christ that is the distinctive mark of his authentic followers.'[19]

Church unity and Christians who dwell in God combine to form a proclamation to the world (as in those who do not know God): Jesus was sent by God and God loves them. There are stories of Jesus appearing to people in visions and dreams, of those who have never set eyes on a Christian and yet find the Way, the Truth and the Life. But those are the exceptions. The rule is that we who believe, by our lives and our relationships with one another, draw people to – or should I say into – Christ.

Jesus knew full well that as fallen humans we would struggle to reach partial, let alone full, unity. However, over 20 centuries later, the majority hold firm to the beliefs captured in the Nicene Creed formally adopted all the way back in 381. We all believe that Jesus Christ is the Son of God, that he was died, buried and on the third day he rose again. And we continue to see new believers added to our number.

For reflection

What experience have you had of seeing the authentic faith of Christians and a unified church draw people to Christ? What part could you play in making this happen more often?

Prayer

Lord Jesus, thank you that you prayed for the believers of the future. Thank you for the example of oneness we see in the relational unity of the Trinity. We are sorry for the disagreements and division we ourselves have been part of. Please help us to have your vision and understanding of the power of unity, and may we remain rooted and established in your love. Amen.

Hermit butterfly *Chazara briseis*

In the hills above Nice, A Rocha studies the little-known hermit butterfly, whose populations are in sharp decline. Since 2000, it has disappeared from 72% of French territory – but the population at Domaine des Courmettes is remarkable!

Day 26

The mind of Christ

Therefore if you have any encouragement from being united with Christ, if any comfort from his love, if any common sharing in the Spirit, if any tenderness and compassion, then make my joy complete by being like-minded, having the same love, being one in spirit and of one mind. Do nothing out of selfish ambition or vain conceit. Rather, in humility value others above yourselves, not looking to your own interests but each of you to the interests of the others.
In your relationships with one another, have the same mindset as Christ Jesus:

> **who, being in very nature God,**
> **did not consider equality with God something to be used to his own advantage.**

PHILIPPIANS 2:1–6

I once complimented someone on the cross he was wearing around his neck. He hurriedly tucked it out of sight under his shirt, saying that he didn't like it to be seen, as his faith was private and personal. He's not the only one choosing to keep his religion on the down low, but the apostle Paul wouldn't recognise the concept of a lone, secretive believer. Those who are 'united with Christ' are by default part of a community of those also united with him. In practice this means belonging to a church, meeting together to share bread and wine, worship, pray and study scripture, caring for one another in practical ways and facing out to the world to bring in the lost, bind up the wounded and plead the cause of the oppressed.

Church can be a long way from ideal. Many, including me, have had some of their most painful interactions with fellow church members. There are endless stories of power-crazed pastors, bad music, impenetrable cliques, boring sermons, not enough emphasis on whatever it is the person telling the story thinks is the most important thing for churches to emphasise… I absolutely agree with you if you consider it easier to opt out. But if you are committed to Jesus, I don't believe he gives you that option.

Relationships between believers are the crucible for spiritual refining, and as we saw yesterday, play a key role in demonstrating God's love for the world. Growing more like Christ means we relate to each other in a countercultural way, a counter-intuitive way, a way that follows in the Lord's steps and not where our feet would naturally take us.

I grew up in A Rocha's first field study centre, a big farmhouse called Cruzinha in southern Portugal. As well as my family of six, the house could hold a good number of others who would sometimes be part of the permanent team and stay several years, sometimes be there to volunteer for a few weeks or months, and sometimes be visiting for a few days. My mum wrote this about the challenges of life in community:

> I quickly discovered that by far the most agonising emotional challenge was produced not by the blatant faults and failures of others but by my own acutely uncomfortable reactions to them… The Bible says, 'if it is possible, *as far as it depends on you*, be at peace with everyone' (Romans 12:18). We can't change the other person – they are always going to be irritating and hard to get on with – but we are responsible for being changed ourselves. As G.K. Chesterton wrote in a letter to *The Times*, 'What's wrong with the world? Dear Sir, I am. Yours sincerely.' All of us are works of art in progress, pots on the wheel, and as with any artistic enterprise one often seems to go backwards not forwards creating more mess instead of the longed-for order.[20]

We have been considering the different relational axes impacted by the cross, starting with how it transformed how we relate to God. The moment Jesus died, the enormous, heavy curtain hiding the altar was ripped top to bottom. As it says in Hebrews: 'By one sacrifice he has made perfect forever those who are being made holy', and ever since we can 'have confidence to enter the Most Holy Place' (Hebrews 10:14, 19).

Close proximity to our heavenly Father brings encouragement, and we receive comfort from his love (v. 1), which is then our gift to pass on. Living alongside Jesus, in the power of the Holy Spirit, his example of humility and sacrifice is constantly before us. It is inevitable that our relationship with God will change our relationships with each other, sometimes unintentionally and simply because of our spiritual transformation; sometimes requiring painful effort and great discipline.

For reflection

Is God challenging you to live more for the interests of others? What practical implications might that have?

Prayer

Lord, I want to have the same mindset as you in my attitude to others but I have a long way to go. I confess I wrestle with a good amount of selfish ambition and vain conceit. I'm sorry. Thank you that your work in me continues. Please help me love my sisters and brothers in your family as you love me and them. Amen.

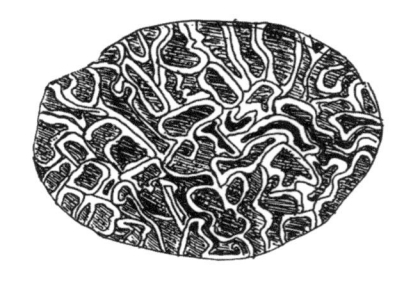

Crisp pillow coral *Anomastraea irregularis*

A Rocha works to study, protect and restore marine habitats. In Kenya, this includes rockpools, important for their diverse habitats and rare, endemic species such as the crisp pillow coral (listed as vulnerable).

Day 27

Unity and diversity

Just as a body, though one, has many parts, but all its many parts form one body, so it is with Christ. For we were all baptised by one Spirit so as to form one body – whether Jews or Gentiles, slave or free – and we were all given the one Spirit to drink. And so the body is not made up of one part but of many.

Now if the foot should say, 'Because I am not a hand, I do not belong to the body,' it would not for that reason stop being part of the body. And if the ear should say, 'Because I am not an eye, I do not belong to the body,' it would not for that reason stop being part of the body. If the whole body were an eye, where would the sense of hearing be? If the whole body were an ear, where would the sense of smell be? But in fact God has placed the parts in the body, every one of them, just as he wanted them to be. If they were all one part, where would the body be? As it is, there are many parts, but one body.
1 CORINTHIANS 12:12–20

The body metaphor is working hard here – well done muscles! – and manages to illustrate two different matters relating to how Christ reset the dynamic among believers. We will look at these one at a time and then see if we can fuse them back together into one body of thought.

The first matter is that baptism by the Spirit removes previously unthinkably deep divides, two of which are mentioned here (Jews and Gentiles, slave and free), with a third added into the mix in Galatians (male and female, see Galatians 3:28). God himself called the

Jews to be separate and gave them their identity as a chosen nation, 'a people holy to the Lord your God' (Deuteronomy 7:6). To now think of themselves as part of the same body as Gentiles, non-Jews, was radically challenging for Jewish Christians. Free people literally owned slaves. In the terms of our metaphor, a free person was like the body and the slave their muddy boots. Now believers are being asked not just to think of themselves as equal humans but as equal as one part of one body is to another.

It is hard to find a parallel that would even give us a hint of how fundamental a shift this was. Perhaps a white person who grew up in the segregationist south of the USA and was an adult during integration might understand the rewiring of neural pathways involved in something like this. You have always been taught you and those like you need to stay away from those like them. You drink from different water sources, you are educated in different schools, you travel in different sections of public transport, and you believe you have an intrinsic right to the better versions of all these. And then your world changes. You no longer have higher status because of your pigmentation. You are all American citizens – one nation. Jesus reset the boundaries of the kingdom. Citizenship is granted through the Holy Spirit, not religious lineage or social standing or nationality or any of the multitudes of other categories we use to subdivide humanity. We are united by our baptism and because we drink of 'one Spirit' (v. 13).

The second matter is that within this body, there is enormous diversity. Our differences are not a problem; in fact, they are essential to our effectiveness, even survival. More than that, God placed the parts 'just as he wanted them to be' (v. 18). We need to have all this spelled out because our natural tendency is to compare ourselves to others, either resulting in pride or insecurity. And often we are more comfortable huddling like sheep with other sheep – one big woolly, white blob in the field.

When I first joined A Rocha, I thought my job was to communicate about the work my very impressive teammates were doing to protect, restore, study and care for vulnerable species and habitats. They were doing nature conservation, and I was just talking about it. Then one day I had one of those conversations that picks you up and sets you down facing a different direction altogether. My boss at the time was a world-renowned conservation scientist who had recently been awarded a global prize for his work on the game-changing IUCN Red List. Simon Stuart didn't fit the mould of impressive conservationist in my mind, he *was* the mould. We were sitting around at the end of a team meeting, and he was probably telling me something about an endangered amphibian when I disclosed how very impotent and unimportant I felt in the face of such enormous numbers of species on the verge of extinction. He told me that I *am* a conservationist. I may not be up to my knees in mud uprooting invasive species of pondweed on a daily basis, or teaching Ugandan school children how to grow food in recycled sacks, or writing influential papers in the journal *Nature* that will lead to new approaches to energy generation, but communicators are important and necessary to the conservation effort. So are business people, artists, politicians, farmers and financiers. One body, many parts, all adding value.

So to put things together: for those of us united in Christ, division is a nonsense. He has made us belong together as completely as if we were one single person. And for that reason, each of us belongs, makes a valued contribution and has a place in the whole that God himself gave us.

For reflection

What is your place in the body of Christ? Do you have an appropriate sense of worth?

Prayer

Thank you, Christ Jesus, God the Father, Holy Spirit, for your oneness and your three-ness. I will never be able to fully understand how both those things are true, but I am grateful for the way you show me what unity and diversity can look like in your church. Help me play my part for the good of the whole. Amen.

Camphor thyme *Thymus Camphoratus*

A Rocha Portugal's discovery of the presence of this protected plant species had a major impact on their court case to stop illegal development of the Ria de Alvor estuary.

Day 28

Obedient love

> And so we know and rely on the love God has for us.
> God is love. Whoever lives in love lives in God, and God in them. This is how love is made complete among us so that we will have confidence on the day of judgement: in this world we are like Jesus. There is no fear in love. But perfect love drives out fear, because fear has to do with punishment. The one who fears is not made perfect in love.
> We love because he first loved us. Whoever claims to love God yet hates a brother or sister is a liar. For whoever does not love their brother and sister, whom they have seen, cannot love God, whom they have not seen. And he has given us this command: anyone who loves God must also love their brother and sister.
> 1 JOHN 4:16–21

I will be open with you and admit I have wrestled with this passage, and specifically these words from verse 20: 'Whoever claims to love God yet hates a brother or sister is a liar.' I claim to love God. Over the course of my life, fellow Christians have hurt me, hurt those I love, behaved in ways that horrify and repulse me. I have had feelings towards these brothers and sisters that could accurately be labelled hate-adjacent at best. Is my claim to love God a lie? Is yours? Thankfully there is a hopeful and grace-filled way across what might seem the impossible challenging waters of verse 21.

Let's start by hopping on to the first stepping stone and rewinding to the beginning of our lives in Christ, our rebirth. 1 John 3 starts out with amazed gratitude that we can say we are children of God because 'that is what we are!' (3:1). We who are reborn in God share his nature. This is a statement of fact not aspiration. A newborn baby has the DNA of their biological mother and father: they don't have to grow into shared characteristics by observing and imitating their parents. The coming of Jesus caused seismic change: a new creation, existing within the old and one day to subsume it. God's grand proclamation through the prophet Isaiah, 'I am doing a new thing!' (Isaiah 43:19), Jesus did. And it forms our identity as a new people of God.

The next stepping stone is a reminder that God's nature – which we now share – is love: 'God is love' (v. 16). As new creations in him, we have his loving heart in place of our own. The connection between us and God forms the connection we have with each other. He loves us, so as those with his nature we love each other. As fish ought to swim, birds fly and mammals have warm blood, so Christians ought to love. It is one of the main ways we can be identified.

The last stepping stone takes us close enough to the far bank to make it all the way over. The love we have for each other is *his* love, and the manifestation of his love is the laying down of himself as God the Son (1 John 3:16; 4:9–10), which neatly takes us to the next place to step.

What does this love we've been talking about look like? The command to love in 1 John is not a command to have fuzzy, warm, giddy feelings about someone. Anyone married for longer than ten minutes will testify that those feelings come and go. Love here is not about emotions but about action. We can't choose to like everything about someone or to agree with all they say or to crave their company. We can choose to give them a lift to a hospital appointment, drop a meal round, help them out financially and so on. The more loving we are, the more like Christ we become.

In situations where it feels impossible to love a Christian brother or sister, we can first remember that with God all things are possible (Matthew 19:26), and then we can ask ourselves: what does hate do? And what does love do? That is the way to the far bank.

For reflection

Have you had anyone in mind while you were reading just now? In what ways could you love them?

Prayer

Thank you, God, that you loved us first. Thank you that your love is lived and expressed in the person of Jesus and his life, death and resurrection. I want to love you truthfully and to live recognisably as your child. I need your help to do that. Amen.

European pond terrapin *Emys orbicularis*

In 2020, A Rocha France led an innovative study of the pond terrapin populations resident in the Natura 2000 site, Marais de la Vallée des Baux, where A Rocha has been working since 1999.

Day 29

Running the race

> **Therefore, since we are surrounded by such a great cloud of witnesses, let us throw off everything that hinders and the sin that so easily entangles. And let us run with perseverance the race marked out for us, fixing our eyes on Jesus, the pioneer and perfecter of faith. For the joy that was set before him he endured the cross, scorning its shame, and sat down at the right hand of the throne of God. Consider him who endured such opposition from sinners, so that you will not grow weary and lose heart.**
> HEBREWS 12:1–3

Sport is a source of great analogies, which is really the only thing about it I appreciate! Here, the spiritual life is framed as a race, which works well as an easily accessible metaphor for people today who run – or maybe prefer to watch – races. It becomes all the richer, however, with a little bit of cultural context.

The four sports festivals collectively known as the Panhellenic Games were one of the ways the Greeks measured time, with the Olympics serving as the starting point for a regular four-year cycle. The festivals were highly religious; each one was celebrated in honour of a god to whom sacrifices would be given. They were occasions where power deals were brokered, political issues thrashed out, alliances made and broken. Some argue that sport is the religion of our age. Looking at the worshipful faces and songs of a winning side's fans in a packed stadium, considering the £39 billion generated each year for the UK economy,[21] the pilgrimages across the world to attend big events, the blood, sweat and tears devoted to specific muscle groups – many a pastor would be glad and possibly surprised to encounter such fervour in the pews. However seriously we take sport, though, Hellenic antiquity was on a whole other level, making a race a brilliant picture for the spiritual life.

Participants in the games came from all over the Greek world, but only the wealthy could afford the training and expenses. Women and non-Greeks were barred from taking part. So here is another opportunity to appreciate the stunningly wide-open welcome of God. I'm reminded of standing before team captains more times in my younger school days than I could count as they fought over who had to take me, the only one left. My desire to be in the team would have been enough with Jesus as team captain. Everyone is welcome to this race and qualified for the prize (which in the Panhellenic Games would have been a wreath of branches and some glory for your home town).

To be sure, you were totally unimpeded; with the exception of chariot racers, all competitors in the games would remove all their clothing. Yes, these sportsmen would be buck naked! Now when you read 'throw off everything that hinders' (v. 1), you'll have to be careful to watch where your mind goes... Once down to their birthday suits, they would rub themselves in olive oil to which the dust of the arena would stick. Archaeologists have often found an instrument known as a strigil at amphitheatres and bathhouses around the Greco-Roman world. This is a curved bronze tool designed for scraping dirt from the skin. Hebrews' first readers would have known just how grubby people would get in the games and been grateful again for the sanctifying grace of God, who cleanses us from our sin and makes us pure and spotless in his sight.

Held in huge stadiums, competitions would have been watched by a 'great cloud of witnesses'. Our witnesses are those who, having lived in faith, have died before us, some named in Hebrews 11, like Abraham, Moses and David, but so many more, known to you and to me. People who taught us who God is, lived like Jesus, sacrificed cheerfully in the power of the Holy Spirit. They serve as our inspiration, our cheerleaders, our accountability.

The footraces were the only event of any length in the games. To be successful, the athlete not only needed to be fast and strong but also gritty. They needed to be able to push through pain and fatigue: to 'run with perseverance' and to 'endure' (vv. 1–2). Jesus overcame the suffering of his race – the cross, the shame – for the joy at the finish line. As we run, we could easily be discouraged by how hard it is to be a Christian and how many of our fellow runners are giving up. That's why Hebrews urges us to fix our eyes on Jesus. He did this ahead of us. He's waiting for us with the crown of new life. It is all worth it.

For reflection

How is your race going? What are you enduring? What is keeping you going? Who is cheering you on from the stands?

Prayer

Jesus, you pioneered a perfectly run race. You are ahead of me, and when I remember to focus on you and not everything around me, my energy and determination rises. You know how hard it can be to keep going. Forgive me for getting tangled up, slowed down and diverted. By your Spirit, may I run my race to the end and join you with the Father for all eternity. Amen.

Kentish plover *Charadrius alexandrinus*

A Rocha Portugal measured the behaviour and breeding success of Kentish plovers from 1990–2005. The presence of breeding Kentish plovers and other rare species important for conservation in the Alvor Estuary has supported the case to protect this unique area.

Day 30

Mercy mixed with fear

> But you, dear friends, by building yourselves up in your most holy faith and praying in the Holy Spirit, keep yourselves in God's love as you wait for the mercy of our Lord Jesus Christ to bring you to eternal life.
> Be merciful to those who doubt; save others by snatching them from the fire; to others show mercy, mixed with fear – hating even the clothing stained by corrupted flesh.
> To him who is able to keep you from stumbling and to present you before his glorious presence without fault and with great joy – to the only God our Saviour be glory, majesty, power and authority, through Jesus Christ our Lord, before all ages, now and forevermore! Amen.
> JUDE 20–25

For those who believe in Jesus as the Messiah, no relationship is untouched by the cross. It forges the strongest of bonds between Jesus-followers, setting us on a familial footing with those who would otherwise be strangers. It gives us responsibilities towards those new family members. It requires us to love our enemies and forgive as we have been forgiven. So far, so uncontroversial. We may struggle to live into those ideals, but we probably wouldn't argue with the principles.

How about the idea of some people being so corrupt that we should go as far as hating fabric that has touched their skin? What do you make of the instruction, 'To others show mercy, mixed with fear – hating even the clothing stained by corrupted flesh'? (v. 23). Or the fact that Jesus said:

> 'Do you think I came to bring peace on earth? No, I tell you, but division. From now on there will be five in one family divided against each other, three against two and two against three. They will be divided, father against son and son against father, mother against daughter and daughter against mother, mother-in-law against daughter-in-law and daughter-in-law against mother-in-law.'
> LUKE 12:51–53

Does the cross bind us to some and separate us from others? Genesis makes clear that all humanity bears God's image, and 2 Peter 3:9 tells us he wants no one to perish and all to come to repentance. Why then does the Bible in some places encourage division or exclusion? Let's dig into these verses from Jude and hopefully get some clarity.

When it comes to conversion, or 'being saved', a person who has 'holy faith' is both *now* under God's mercy and in his kingdom and *waiting* to be brought to eternal life. There's another pairing of truths we need to hold in tension here too; it is Jesus Christ who brings us to eternal life, and God who keeps us from stumbling and makes us appear faultless in his presence. And yet we have choices, responsibilities and work to do to finish out our race. We must 'build ourselves up', 'pray in the Holy Spirit' and 'keep ourselves in God's love'. The implication is that we can't be casual about our faith. We can't doze off at the wheel because, as I'm sure some bumper sticker somewhere says, 'God's the driver of this car!'

As Christians we need to be aware that while we live in this fallen world, with our fallen desires alive and well, some people are mortally dangerous and, while shown mercy, they are to be feared (v. 23). Specifically, the people to fear are those within the community of faith who by words and conduct entice us to a false gospel and thus jeopardise our standing with God. The letter of Jude was instigated by the fact that a group of believers had been infiltrated by some individuals who were arguing the grace of God provides licence for sexual immorality and that Jesus is not the only Saviour (v. 4). These people present a threat because both those positions are attractive and lead down an easier path, following natural instincts. Jude is blunt about where this ends: in condemnation (v. 4), destruction (vv. 5, 10–11), judgement (v. 6) and blackest darkness (v. 13).

We aren't to form hygienic bubbles of the saved, hermetically sealed away from the great contaminating unwashed. But the cross has given us a gift of incalculable worth – eternal life in God's presence. No human relationship is worth putting that at risk, so if we become aware that a particular person is undermining our faith, the way of wisdom is to get some distance from them.

For reflection

How do you 'build yourself up in faith'?

Prayer

Lord God, you are majestic, powerful, merciful and loving. Thank you for the cross. By the Holy Spirit, keep me strong and focused on you in this life of faith. Help me discern my relationships wisely so that I am not under dangerous influences. Amen.

Clarke's weaver *Ploceus golandi*

The Kenyan-endemic Clarke's weaver is one of the rarest birds in the world. Its breeding sites had never been found – until 2013, when A Rocha found a colony in the Dakatcha Woodland, now an A Rocha nature reserve.

IV

People and creation

CHARLES FOSTER has connected with the natural world at a deeper level than most. He has lived as up close and personal as humanly possibly with a variety of wild creatures – rustling around in the mud eating worms in his badger phase, wild swimming and sniffing poo as an otter, and not only growing out his toenails and hair in solidarity with red deer but requesting a friend to unleash his hounds so he could share the experience of being hunted.[22] While identifying as an urban fox, he had a close encounter as his chicken leg was being thieved. 'I felt not just that I was looking and observing,' he said, 'but that I was being looked at and being observed. That was the reciprocity I had longed for. I don't feel I got that anywhere else.'[23]

At the other end of the spectrum are the estimated one million Japanese *hikikomori* – individuals who have spent months or years at a time in self-imposed isolation in a single room in their parents' homes.[24] And the gamers who live largely virtual lives. And residents of Dubai, which with 2% of green space is the world's most concreted urban space.[25]

Whether we are more of a *hikikomori* or a Charles Foster, all of us live in an interdependent relationship with the rest of creation. Even our bodies are complex ecosystems – vibrant communities of trillions of tiny beings – bacteria, viruses and fungi. According to the American Museum of Natural History:

> As they have changed over time, microbes and humans have formed complex relationships with each other. Humans need microbes to stay healthy, and microbes need the environments provided by the human body to survive.[26]

As the cross resets and transforms our relationship with God and with each other, so it does our relationship with the non-human creation. In these last ten days of Lent, we will consider how God designed this relationship to work, the impact of sin and brokenness, the calling on us to live in the world in the light of our redemption, and the biblical vision for the new heavens and new earth.

Day 31

The first mission

> Then God said, 'Let us make mankind in our image, in our likeness, so that they may rule over the fish in the sea and the birds in the sky, over the livestock and all the wild animals, and over all the creatures that move along the ground.'
>
> > So God created mankind in his own image,
> > in the image of God he created them;
> > male and female he created them.
>
> God blessed them and said to them, 'Be fruitful and increase in number; fill the earth and subdue it. Rule over the fish in the sea and the birds in the sky and over every living creature that moves on the ground.'
>
> GENESIS 1:26–28

If I asked you to do a brain dump of all the instructions from God found in the Bible you can think of in one minute, your list might include a good few of the ten commandments, the first bit of what is known as 'the great commission' ('Go and make disciples of all nations', Matthew 28:19), and maybe some of the things Jesus said during his last supper about love and serving each other. I wonder how many of us would have written the very first mission God gave us or noticed that it relates not to our fellow humans but to the inhabitants of the sea, the sky and the land. Creation care is not tangential to the life of a Christian. It is woven into our very identity as children of God, and is therefore as integral to the life of faith as prayer, meeting the needs of the poor, meeting together as Christians, tithing and so on.

When it comes to what this mission God gave us looks like, opinions have been divided. In an influential article in the journal *Science* from 1967, Lynn White Jr laid the blame for the emerging ecological crisis on these verses in Genesis.[27] He argued they establish the notion of human domination over creation and legitimise its exploitation and abuse. 'Subdue' and 'rule over': by giving us these instructions, didn't God make us lord and master of all? Is it any wonder we have hunted the majestic blue whale close to extinction, that you'll hear dramatically less birdsong on a woodland walk in England today than you would have as recently as the year White's article was published, or that cattle and sheep are likely to be the only creatures moving along the ground you'll see in our countryside?

Taking a word or a phrase in isolation from its textual context generally does violence to its meaning, and here is a perfect example of why it is bad practice. We have to understand 'rule' and 'subdue' in the light of the rest of the Bible, which makes clear that the 'earth is the Lord's, and everything in it' (Psalm 24:1). Any authority we have is delegated to us and to be exercised within boundaries, with humility, mindful we are earth-keeping on God's behalf, serving him by serving creation. God put his likeness in us 'so that' (v. 26) we may rule in a God-like way. Genesis is not Ground Zero of the environmental catastrophe; it is a beautiful vision for our partnership with God in tending his world for its good.

I would say I'm an average person, coming from a non-science background and engaged in a career that has me locked into quality time with my laptop rather than immersed in nature. But I've learnt from A Rocha a new perspective on the vastness of God's creation, the magnitude of humankind's fall and the need for fellowship and collaboration as we partake in God's redemption plan.

No one knows everything. What would an oceanographer know about the forest? How much does an entomologist know about policies and policymaking towards conservation? Turns out, not much. And this is why creation care requires all hands on deck – not just the 'science people', but also the lawyers, policymakers, marketers, designers, even simply advocators, to work together to care for God's creation.

If all this feels a bit like trying to absorb the distance between stars, perhaps it might help if I told you about Milo and Luna. Milo and Luna are the Swinney family cats, velvety black siblings who came to live with us as kittens. When they reached the appropriate age, we had them neutered so the local cat population wouldn't explode. They wear collars with bells which severely inhibits their hunting game, and we feed them so they don't need mice or birds to stay alive. Now and then they get into scrapes and we take them to the vet if it looks like they aren't healing up as they should. We had to teach them not to jump up on the kitchen counters or the dining room table by spraying them with a water bottle. Human food is tempting for them but not healthy. We do what we can to take care of them responsibly, and I reckon they have a rather blissful life, as it goes. I often think that living so closely alongside another species is a foretaste of heaven and a tangible sign of the kingdom of God here and now.

For reflection

What does creation care look like in your life? What creatures are doing better because of your responsibility for them?

Prayer

Creator God, this world is yours. I'm sorry that I forget that sometimes. You have placed enormous trust in us, and we haven't always ruled in the way you intended us to. I want to do better. By your Holy Spirit, help me be a blessing to your creation. Amen.

Garry oak *Quercus garryana*

Garry oak is the only oak tree native to British Columbia, Canada, and its habitat is very restricted. In the early 2000s, A Rocha helped inventory and oversee restoration on two island sites. In 2015–17, we partnered with Hope Farm on environmental projects, such as restoring 3,000 square metres of Garry oak meadows.

Day 32

Wicked living

> How long will the land lie parched
>   and the grass in every field be withered?
> Because those who live in it are wicked,
>   the animals and birds have perished.
> Moreover, the people are saying,
>   'He will not see what happens to us'…
>
> 'Many shepherds will ruin my vineyard
>   and trample down my field;
> they will turn my pleasant field
>   into a desolate wasteland.
> It will be made a wasteland,
>   parched and desolate before me;
> the whole land will be laid waste
>   because there is no one who cares.'
>
> JEREMIAH 12:4, 10–11

There is story we like to tell ourselves about how with each new generation, humans get better. C.S. Lewis called it 'chronological snobbery'. My teenage daughters (who are wonderful and, incidentally, a persuasive argument for the progress narrative) can barely imagine the pre-smart phone, social media, personal computer world into which I was born, where you got information from libraries, made plans far in advance and had to keep to them, and needed to go to a shop with physical money to get things. They certainly live in a world with better healthcare, education and opportunities for women than those in Jeremiah's time.

They have also had to deal with cyberbullying, repeated ambulance dashes to the hospital thanks to lungs coated with London grime and a global pandemic from which they were compelled to hide in our home for months at a time. The world in the 2020s may have improved in certain regards but the human heart has the same dark tendencies it did in Medieval times or the Stone Age, and much of our suffering as a species remains self-inflicted.

The prophet Jeremiah's questions are rhetorical here, and I'm sure that even in his wildest nightmares he would never have seen what was coming beyond his lifetime. However terrible the drought in the late seventh century BC in Judah, the scale of extinction, desertification and changing weather patterns is of a different order now. How long will the land lie parched because of the wicked living there? A very long time, as it turns out.

That is because how we behave towards land, grass, animals and birds is an expression of our beliefs about the world and our place in it. A world view is not an abstract, cerebral philosophy; it is rubber tyres on tarmac roads. At a national level, hospice care or euthanasia, child labour or full-time education, respect for borders or military invasions – these are societal world views in action. If I believe the world is but a stage, storehouse and slagheap for the great human drama, I am going to have no concern at all about how it fares beyond its ability to fulfil those functions. That is putting things more starkly than most people would recognise. However, this sentiment – a quote from the internet I am including unattributed as I do not want to shame an individual – is widespread: 'We ought to love and care for the earth because we must care for the most vulnerable people on the planet.' The belief that the earth only matters because people matter (especially the poor) is one I've heard expressed many, many times. It would lead to creation care, but only if that aspect of creation could demonstrate its benefit to humans.

Jeremiah rightly draws a line directly from 'the wicked' to the dry grass and dying creatures. The desolation of the land is 'because there is no one who cares' (v. 11). With each passing century we've grown better at enriching ourselves from 'natural resources' which we think of as ours to use freely. We've had no regard for our children or grandchildren, eating, drinking and making merry, because 'tomorrow we die' (Isaiah 22:13). Never mind others will have to find a way to live in the mess we've made or the fact none of it belongs to us – note God's words in verse 10: '*My* vineyard... *my* field' (emphasis mine).

Our sins and idolatry are not private matters. They have expressed themselves in the extinction of the Tasmanian tiger and the great auk, in the toxicity of the Salton Sea and the erosion of the Kuril Islands' soil. Gus Speth, a lawyer and former US advisor on climate, said:

> I used to think that the top environmental problems were biodiversity loss, ecosystem collapse and climate change. I thought that 30 years of good science could address these problems. I was wrong. The top environmental problems are selfishness, greed and apathy. To deal with these, we need a cultural and spiritual transformation. And we lawyers and scientists don't know how to do that.[28]

The ecological crisis has spiritual roots, and unless we address the problem of the human heart nothing will change.

For reflection

What are your true beliefs about the earth? Do you need a change of heart?

Prayer

Creator God, I am sorry for my wrong beliefs and the harmful actions they have led to. Thank you for your grace and forgiveness. Help me to live in right relationship with all living things in this world of yours. Amen.

White-throated dipper *Cinclus cinclus*

In the Czech Republic, A Rocha is monitoring dipper populations, which have come under threat through extreme weather conditions and acidic pollution.

Day 33

Consequences

'Will a mere mortal rob God? Yet you rob me.
   'But you ask, "How are we robbing you?"
   'In tithes and offerings. You are under a curse – your whole nation – because you are robbing me. Bring the whole tithe into the storehouse, that there may be food in my house. Test me in this,' says the Lord Almighty, 'and see if I will not throw open the floodgates of heaven and pour out so much blessing that there will not be room enough to store it. I will prevent pests from devouring your crops, and the vines in your fields will not drop their fruit before it is ripe,' says the Lord Almighty. 'Then all the nations will call you blessed, for yours will be a delightful land,' says the Lord Almighty.
MALACHI 3:8–12

This is a fun passage for showing how easy it is to draw false conclusions from snippets of the Bible. Let me demonstrate. Based on these verses alone, we could argue God only owns a fraction of what we have: the Israelites were stealing from God in withholding their tithes, ergo the tithe part is the bit belonging to God and not the rest. We might also conclude that prosperity preachers urging hearers to give generously – to them usually – as a financial investment are only taking God at his word (v. 10). And we could come away thinking pests and crop failures are a direct result of failure to give a percentage of our income, on a national level, to the church. God, through Malachi, seems to be describing a dysfunctional triangulation whereby conflict between human and divine is mediated via issues between human and the rest of creation. We don't give God back what is his? Fine. He will let the bugs loose on the barley.

As I said at the outset, all those are false conclusions. Tithing is a symbolic reminder that *everything* we have is God's; being a faithful giver is definitely not a guarantee of personal wealth, and unripe grapes are not a direct result of sin. What, then, are the truths at the heart of these puzzling verses?

Firstly, once again we have an opportunity to check our perspective. Have we fallen into thinking we are the centre of the universe, lords and masters of all? Our influence over the world is circumscribed. We put seeds into the ground, we pull out weeds and put in fertiliser, we harvest and process and consume. We do not generate matter; rather, we work with what God has created. We cannot divide cells and cause life or growth. We are at the mercy of the weather, neither able to make it rain or hold back wind. God alone can 'throw open the floodgates of heaven' to bless us; 'the wind and the waves obey him' (Matthew 8:27) and we are at their mercy.

Secondly, the language of curse and blessing is covenantal. Malachi was an Old Testament prophet, in a time of particular binding agreements between God and his chosen nation. The covenants came with consequences for keeping them (blessings) and for breaking them (curses). God's desire in relating to his creation is always to bless. That comes across loud and clear in these verses. The Lord Almighty is yearning for Israel to do the right thing, so that their land will be delightful and a beacon of hope to 'all the nations' (v. 12).

Thirdly, in some ways these verses are simply presenting the reality that when we have a disordered and broken relationship with God, at both individual and societal levels, our relationship with creation breaks down as a result. As with an ecosystem, every part needs to work together for the survival and health of the whole. I can't think of a better illustration of this than the Great Sparrow War in China.

Mao Zedong was the first chairman of the People's Republic of China. He led his people into Communism believing it the most effective route to prosperity. As an atheist, there was no higher power than himself involved in shaping his policies towards the natural world, some of which were frankly mind-boggling. Take this one. As part of his Great Leap Forward initiative, a law was passed in 1959 requiring citizens to assist in the elimination of sparrows. Sparrows, he declared, were enemies of Communism and stood in the way of progress, stealing grain and benefiting from the labour of the proletariat. Over a period of three years, nests were destroyed, eggs smashed, saucepans bashed to frighten and exhaust them, and these defenceless little birds were hunted down and destroyed to the brink of extinction. Approximately one billion were slaughtered. However, instead of saving the country four pounds of rice per year per bird, in decimating sparrows Mao had removed the control on the locust population, thus precipitating an ecological crisis that was one of the main factors in the deaths of an estimated 55 million people from starvation. In cursing this species, Mao cursed his own.

This is God's world, and it works best when we live in it as he intended, seeking the good of the whole, of which we are just one part.

For reflection

Spend some time mulling over these words about Jesus from Colossians 1:17: 'In him all things hold together.' Try to absorb the scope of their implications.

Prayer

> In Matthew 10:29, Jesus says God cares about a single sparrow falling to the ground. From the small and insignificant to us, the crowning glory of his creation, God sees and loves all he has made. Ask him to help you see and love the world as he does.

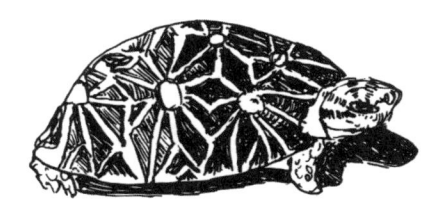

Geometric tortoise *Psammobates geometricus*

South Africa is home to 14 terrestrial tortoise species – the largest diversity of tortoise species of any country in the world. Many are threatened and poorly known. A Rocha is partnering with FreeMe Wildlife to create a dedicated tortoise rehabilitation and reintroduction programme.

Day 34

All creatures of our God

He makes grass grow for the cattle,
    and plants for people to cultivate –
    bringing forth food from the earth:
wine that gladdens human hearts,
    oil to make their faces shine,
    and bread that sustains their hearts.
The trees of the Lord are well watered,
    the cedars of Lebanon that he planted.
There the birds make their nests;
    the stork has its home in the junipers.
The high mountains belong to the wild goats;
    the crags are a refuge for the hyrax.

He made the moon to mark the seasons,
    and the sun knows when to go down.
You bring darkness, it becomes night,
    and all the beasts of the forest prowl.
The lions roar for their prey
    and seek their food from God.
The sun rises, and they steal away;
    they return and lie down in their dens.
PSALM 104:14–22

Spoiler alert: in the black comedy film *Triangle of Sadness*,[29] a luxury cruise is comprehensively disrupted by a deranged alcoholic captain, food poisoning, a storm and a pirate attack. When a grenade blows up the ship, seven survivors wash up on a tropical shore. Where mega wealth had previously given the cruise passengers every advantage in life and thus a belief in their own inherent superiority, the formerly privileged castaways now find themselves inadequate to the challenges of wilderness survival. Abigail, erstwhile housekeeper, is soon able to gain power with her octopus-hunting skills. The former servant becomes the master. For her, and for us as viewers, it is deliciously satisfying to witness the hierarchy upended.

The way of wisdom is to heed parables and amend our ways accordingly. *Triangle of Sadness* signposts the foolishness of denying our common humanity. From the comfort of your armchair, you can watch an oligarch, a weapons manufacturer, a tech millionaire and a couple of pampered supermodels cut down to size without having to live through your own shipwreck life lesson to learn we are all naked under our clothes.

As the wealthy cruisers in *Triangle of Sadness* had advantages of money, power and sex appeal, so *Homo sapiens* have an elevated position in creation as God's image bearers. While this primarily confers upon us greater responsibility and labour, the danger is we instead come to behave like entitled brats.

Psalm 104 reminds us we are creatures among other creatures – all of us dependent on our maker. We may prefer to focus on our elevated position but let's not forget that, like the cattle, we rely on God for food; like the trees, we need the divinely instated water purification systems of the biosphere; we are utterly dependent along with all other living things on the provision of the sun's energy. Even our relative strengths of mental prowess and dexterity only help us in certain contexts. God gave dominion to each species so that peaceful coexistence is possible. If you were to wander a remote forest at night, a hungry beast would easily put you in your place.

We as humans are part of creation. Creation as a whole is both dependent on God and a recipient of his loving provision. When we consider the incarnation and the sacrificial death of Jesus, we are missing a massive part of the picture by only looking at the bit where he came to rescue people from sin. That is there in the frame, but so too is his eternal love for and pleasure in the cedar, the stork, the hyrax, the mountain goat and the lion. Let's stand back and expand our perspective. Let's see ourselves in situ, in the glorious whole, in a world revolving around God Almighty, not us.

For reflection

Look back at these verses from Psalm 104 and pay attention to all the interactions between God and the non-human creation. What strikes you?

Prayer

Lord God, I confess to arrogance and self-centredness. I forget I am a creature among creatures, utterly dependent on you and at your mercy. Thank you for your love for me, for all people and for the whole creation. Please forgive me and put me in my proper place. Amen.

Kelp *Laminaria digitata*

A Rocha UK researched the impact of blue-rayed limpets on the forests of kelp in bays near Lee Abbey, Devon. On Lee Bay itself, over 90 different intertidal species and 17 different habitats were identified.

Day 35

Learning from the lilies

'Therefore I tell you, do not worry about your life, what you will eat or drink; or about your body, what you will wear. Is not life more than food, and the body more than clothes? Look at the birds of the air; they do not sow or reap or store away in barns, and yet your heavenly Father feeds them. Are you not much more valuable than they? Can any one of you by worrying add a single hour to your life?

'And why do you worry about clothes? See how the flowers of the field grow. They do not labour or spin. Yet I tell you that not even Solomon in all his splendour was dressed like one of these. If that is how God clothes the grass of the field, which is here today and tomorrow is thrown into the fire, will he not much more clothe you – you of little faith?'
MATTHEW 6:25–30

I began working with A Rocha International in June 2020. Our team is spread around the world, and we have no central office, so it was always going to be a home-based and largely virtual role. However, thanks to a certain public health issue, even limited in-person contact with my colleagues and our field-based conservation was impossible for the first year and a half of the job. I felt like a brain in a glass jar – disembodied and disconnected from all but my laptop.

The 1999 science fiction classic *The Matrix*[30] postulates an entirely virtual context for static, wired-up humans, an image which continues to horrify me all these years after I saw the film. While it may present (what I choose to believe is) a distant dystopian fantasy, we live in a world of increasing urbanisation, sophisticated digitisation of many of our daily activities, and for many growing separation from nature.

Why does any of that matter? There are lots of answers you could give to that question, but we'll confine ourselves to the scope of Jesus' teaching here on birdwatching and botany. It sits in what is known as 'the sermon on the mount', so we can picture him speaking in the open air, able to gesture to a passing raven or gorgeous little Nazareth iris. He's been talking about money, about how that kind of treasure is liable to be stolen or depleted. He knows full well the human temptation to become enslaved to the pursuit of wealth, how gold can be a god. Underlying the tendency to be mastered by money is anxiety, and so Jesus gets to the heart of the matter. This is a question of trust. 'Little faith' (v. 30) leads to worry about food and clothing, or rather the means to pay for them. How then do we increase faith in God, so that we can serve him with an undivided heart? Be attentive to the birds and the flowers, Jesus says. Learn from their simple reliance on God's care and provision. See how they are fed from great, divinely designed storehouses; see how their finery puts Solomon's fanciest robes in the shade. Rest in acceptance of the limits of your power to cover your own back and meet your own needs and in so doing find freedom from the grip of the need to grow your bank balance.

We don't need to validate the wisdom of God by conducting independent research, but we shouldn't be surprised to see academic studies demonstrate that Jesus knew what he was talking about. A handful of examples: in the Netherlands, there is less mental and physical disease in areas with more green space; in Scotland, primary school children were found to have increasing levels of self-esteem the more access they had to nature; in Italy, undergraduate students recovered faster from mental fatigue in natural environments as compared to urban.[31] Go figure.

For reflection

Find a tree, a patch of sky, a furry, feathered or scaly creature and ask God to sooth your anxiety as you quietly pay attention.

Prayer

Lord, I do worry – a lot – about all sorts of things. Even now my worries are threatening to derail this time of prayer. Open my eyes to the beauty of your world. Calm my anxiety and help me learn from the birds and the lilies how to trust you. Amen.

Black-headed lapwing *Vanellus tectus*

Eden, an A Rocha associated project, monitors the many resident and visiting species at Rennajj Fish Farm, 80 hectares of wetland and savannah on the fringes of Jos, Nigeria.

Day 36

Eyes to see

The wrath of God is being revealed from heaven against all the godlessness and wickedness of people, who suppress the truth by their wickedness, since what may be known about God is plain to them, because God has made it plain to them. For since the creation of the world God's invisible qualities – his eternal power and divine nature – have been clearly seen, being understood from what has been made, so that people are without excuse.

For although they knew God, they neither glorified him as God nor gave thanks to him, but their thinking became futile and their foolish hearts were darkened. Although they claimed to be wise, they became fools and exchanged the glory of the immortal God for images made to look like a mortal human being and birds and animals and reptiles.
ROMANS 1:18–23

I'm a girl who appreciates logic. So I have little patience for the idea that all religions have the same God behind them – the many-roads-to-one-mountain-peak idea – although of course there are genuine seekers of the Divine in every tradition. The world's religions contradict each other on almost all major points, from whether there is one god or millions, or none, how to please a deity, what happens after we die, how the world was made and what help or blessings may be on offer.

As a Christian, I believe God, though invisible, can be clearly seen (v. 20). I realise that sounds illogical, but bear with me! We are going to get a bit epistemological now and dig into how we know what we know, specifically of Yahweh, the Trinity, Alpha and Omega, the one true almighty God. This God desires to be known and has revealed himself in three main ways.

Firstly, in the person of Jesus, 'the image of the invisible God' (Colossians 1:15). Jesus, being God in human form, is relatable to us. He used language we could understand, told stories about recognisable situations, and faced the joys and sufferings familiar to *Homo sapiens* everywhere.

Secondly, in scripture – the 66 books which make up the biblical canon. Through historical narrative, prophecy, poetry, apocalyptic literature, epistles and proverbs, God still speaks today. In my third year of university, I met a fellow student who was looking for Christians having met God by reading through the gospels. He had never been to church or had a conversation with a believer, but the Holy Spirit gave him understanding as he read, and he had been comprehensively converted.

And now we come to today's reading. The creation points to the creator. It speaks of God's power and nature, so anyone and everyone can hear and understand. It 'pours forth speech', as Psalm 19:2 says. This world, in all its beauty, complexity, comedy and majesty, is a loquacious evangelist. People can say they have no interest in God, that they reject his overtures, that they prefer to worship something or someone else, but they can't plead ignorance. God can be known on the basis of the created universe, in which every single person lives or lived or will live. To put it bluntly, as Paul does here, there is no excuse for atheism or idolatry.

The letter goes on to say that, instead of seeing through the window of creation to the God who made it and responding in awe and worship, some people get fixated on the glass. Actually, let's face it: a great many do. Godlessness and wickedness continue to abound, as do futile thinking and foolish hearts. All the sadness and frustration we may feel about this is nothing to God's, who loves all he has made and desires everyone to be saved (see 1 Timothy 2:4; 2 Peter 3:9; Ezekiel 18:23; Matthew 23:37).

For those of us who have seen, heard and responded to the revelation of God in creation, let's continue to study the 'book of works', seeking a greater vision of his power and nature. The more alert and attentive we are to the big and small details of the world, the more our faith will grow.

For reflection

What have you learnt about God from being in nature?

Prayer

Lord God, thank you for being a God who communicates. You are not hidden, silent or absent. I know there are times I look and don't see, even though your glory is evident. And I don't always give you the thanks and the praise you deserve. This world you have made is mind-blowing. You are infinitely brilliant, creative and inventive, expansive and exuberant. Show me more. I will try not to miss it. Amen.

Weaver's fritillary *Boloria dia*

Dry grasslands provide habitat for more than 30% of Switzerland's living species: flowers, butterflies, grasshoppers, reptiles, birds, plants, small mammals and insects like the Weaver's fritillary. These dry grasslands are in steep decline and A Rocha is helping reverse the trend through biodiversity surveys and habitat management.

Day 37

Small mercies

> If you come across a bird's nest beside the road, either in a tree or on the ground, and the mother is sitting on the young or on the eggs, do not take the mother with the young. You may take the young, but be sure to let the mother go, so that it may go well with you and you may have a long life.
> DEUTERONOMY 22:6–7

I have just seen a disturbing viral video showing a McDonald's security guard soaking a homeless man's sleeping bag with his mop as the man sat in it. Shawn, my husband, recently came upon (and challenged, I'm proud to say) a mob of teenage boys tormenting a homeless woman in the middle of our city, Bath, known more for its status as a UNESCO World Heritage site than its violent yobs. In recent times, rough sleepers around the UK have been urinated on, had bricks and beer cans thrown at them, been kicked and even set on fire. A survey carried out by the charity Crisis horrifyingly found as many as eight in ten homeless people had been physically assaulted in some way. What's behind this violence towards one of the world's most downtrodden populations? I'm sure there are many explanations, among them the fact that weak egos need vulnerable targets to increase their sense of power.

There are few more vulnerable targets than a mother bird with young or eggs in her nest. Her fierce instinct to defend her offspring will keep her fixed in place as danger approaches. She could fly out of reach and save herself, but often she won't. And so, there is a decision to be made. We have the power to snuff her out or to let her live and hopefully have more young one day.

Perhaps you are surprised to find a biblical precept making clear God's perspective on what our choice should be. It seems a very small matter to have made it into Old Testament law. In Jewish custom it is known as the least of the commandments. Matthew Henry notes in his commentary on these verses, 'He that let go a bird out of his hand (which was worth two in the bush) purely because God bade him, in that made it to appear that he esteemed all God's precepts concerning all things to be right.'[32]

But there is something more to it than simply a way of testing the degree to which a person is willing to be obedient to anything God might say. It comes with the same promise as the fifth of the ten commandments itself, to honour our fathers and mothers. How we treat a bird in a nest is in some way bound up with blessing and life expectancy. This is clearly significant.

In the very beginning, when God made everything and declared it 'very good', he could trust his image-bearing people to live in the world and care for it as he intended. After the fall, his image remained, but grew blurry and faint – more so in some than others. As the reflection of God in us diminishes, so does our essential humanity. There are some people in whom it has become dim indeed, those who derive pleasure from casual cruelty to the homeless or a wren on her clutch. This little law in Deuteronomy comes just after one commanding people to help a fallen cow or donkey back on its feet. It needed to be said, because the instinct would have been to walk on by, after having a bit of a point, a stare and maybe even a chuckle at the predicament of a mute beast waving its hooves around helplessly in the air.

And so to the Easter story. In his death and resurrection Jesus gave us the chance to get back our humanity in its fullest sense. An aspect of that is to share his deep love and compassion for *every* living thing, great and teeny tiny, showing mercy and kindness indiscriminately as he did. The cross gives us a renewed identity. Integrity means we'll treat nesting birds with care.

For reflection

What small and seemingly insignificant creatures in your neighbourhood could do with your compassion?

Prayer

God of the universe, you made yourself very small in becoming a man. Your concern stretches to a single sparrow and her eggs. I want to be like you in every way, including in this. Amen.

Keeled skimmer *Orthetrum coerulescens*

A Rocha local groups manage sites around the Netherlands: three are Natura 2000 sites and many host species listed on the Dutch IUCN Red List, such as the keeled skimmer dragonfly and the Choleva spadicea, *a species of truffle beetle found for the first time in Gelderland province since 1967 on one of the sites A Rocha manages (French Camp, Bennekom).*

Day 38

Back in our place

'Does the hawk take flight by your wisdom
 and spread its wings towards the south?
Does the eagle soar at your command
 and build its nest on high?
It dwells on a cliff and stays there at night;
 a rocky crag is its stronghold.
From there it looks for food;
 its eyes detect it from afar.
Its young ones feast on blood,
 and where the slain are, there it is.'

The Lord said to Job:

'Will the one who contends with the Almighty correct him?
 Let him who accuses God answer him!'

Then Job answered the Lord:

'I am unworthy – how can I reply to you?
 I put my hand over my mouth.
I spoke once, but I have no answer –
 twice, but I will say no more.'
JOB 39:26—40:5

If one of the great gifts of the incarnation is God stooping to our eye level where we can see him, one of the ways we have most badly misunderstood it is to think we are therefore of the same stature. 'Do not think of yourself more highly than you ought,' says Paul (Romans 12:3), arguably wasting his breath. Because most of us do assess ourselves with overblown generosity, whether in the privacy of our own minds or perhaps a bit more publicly. Donald J. Trump's tweets of 6 January 2018 come to mind:

> Actually, throughout my life, my two greatest assets have been mental stability and being, like, really smart… I went from VERY successful businessman, to top T.V. Star to President of the United States (on my first try). I think that would qualify as not smart, but genius and a very stable genius at that!

Job on social media wouldn't sound too different.

> Unfair. @eliphaz @bildad @zophar liars. I am pure, I have done no wrong, I am clean and free from sin #innocent #whyme #deservebetterfromGod

But by time we get to the passage above, something has changed for Job. What has taken him from talking back to God to covering his mouth with a deep and appropriate sense of unworthiness? What has given him the comfort of laying down the need to understand before accepting his situation? How has he gained a right sense of awe, wonder and fearful respect in the presence of the Almighty? By having his attention drawn to creation: clouds, constellations, clods of earth; wild donkeys, snorting horses, powerful oxen; raging rivers and lotus plants, creatures of the deep oceans and high desert.

Jesus came close to us, walked among us, submitted to the physical limitations of a human's need for food, rest and shelter. He was like us, but he was part of the Godhead too – there before the beginning of all things, at the heart of the creation of matter, on the throne ruling for eternity. We have enormous, unshakable value because he loves us, and we are also tiny and not all that important in the scheme of things. Hawks and eagles will put us back in our place if we pay attention. They migrate, feed and breed without regard to our doings. Birds are far more likely to adapt to and survive the conditions of a changed climate. As the moral theologian Oliver M.T. O'Donovan put it, the vast universe of nature 'makes this proud specimen of our race feel very small. He has no claim to a stable or well-balanced ecosystem in the face of a nature so diverse in its teleologies, so indifferent to human concerns'.[33]

A right relationship with creation becomes a gateway to a right relationship with God. If we can for one second cover our mouths and listen to what nature teaches us about our common creator, we have the opportunity to 'repent, then, and turn to God, so that your sins may be wiped out, that times of refreshing may come from the Lord' (Acts 3:19).

For reflection

Where or what in nature gives you a sense of wonder and makes you feel small? Imagine yourself before it and ask God to use it to give you a more accurate perspective on yourself and him than you have perhaps had until now.

Prayer

Holy Creator God, however often I forget the fact, I know deep down that like Job I am unworthy. And yet you welcome me to come into your presence without fear of rejection because of your Son Jesus Christ. I'm in awe and I worship you now. Amen.

Russell's viper *Daboia russelii*

The Bannerghatta locals have A Rocha India on call to come and remove snakes when found in unexpected places – this helps keep the snakes alive and offers a good teaching moment of the importance of protecting reptiles and the role they play in agricultural ecosystems.

Day 39

Children, wolves and cobras

> The wolf will live with the lamb,
>   the leopard will lie down with the goat,
> the calf and the lion and the yearling together;
>   and a little child will lead them.
> The cow will feed with the bear,
>   their young will lie down together,
>   and the lion will eat straw like the ox.
> The infant will play near the cobra's den,
>   and the young child will put its hand into the viper's nest.
> They will neither harm nor destroy
>   on all my holy mountain,
> for the earth will be filled with the knowledge of the Lord
>   as the waters cover the sea.
>
> ISAIAH 11:6–9

The story of God and humanity is often told in four great acts: creation, fall, redemption, new creation. In a few devastating beats, Genesis takes us from a perfectly harmonious ecosystem to an antagonistic power struggle between all living things: men and women hide from their maker; men throughout history have oppressed women; snakes and people have never done well in close proximity; and our dominion has often been exercised as animal cruelty and abuse. Just because we can produce chickens to eat cheaply and fast, if we cram them into warehouses and ignore their suffering, doesn't mean that we should.

In Christ came redemption, the inauguration of a new era. The kingdom of God is present wherever and whenever his will is done on earth as in heaven. As citizens, we strive to live out our relationships with our king, each other and his world according to his intention. On our best days, we shine with the very light of heaven, like stars in the sky (Philippians 2:15).

However, we continue to live in a world where wolves sink their teeth into lambs and a toddler in a viper's nest would meet a quick and nasty end. Old hostilities remain. There is enmity between species and individuals everywhere you look. Only last night, my sweet fluffy kitties turned on each other out of nowhere and had to be pulled apart before they racked up some serious vet bills. Think hippos look cute? They kill up to 3,000 people every year.

The final act is yet to begin, but here the prophet Isaiah paints a picture of what it will look like. The scene is somewhat familiar. It is our world, albeit significantly transformed. This is a richly biodiverse earth and not a planet scraped of all but *Homo sapiens* souls, as the afterlife is sometimes imagined to be. Can you think of anything drearier?

The new creation is saturated with 'the knowledge of the Lord as the waters cover the sea' (v. 9). The sea *is* water! And the whole cosmos will be, in the same state-the-obvious sense, imbued with God's love. God's love will soak every stain, every threat, every harm out of existence, such that the very nature of all living things is changed. Predator and prey will set up home together. Children wander around in perfect safety. The curse of Genesis 3:15 will be definitively lifted.

I wonder if you have logistical questions about heaven. I know I do. Will we all be the same age or will there be children and young creatures? Will we all be herbivores? Will there be a finite number of creatures or will the cycle of birth, life and death continue for some species? How will the space/time continuum work and where will everyone live? A passage like this one in Isaiah is not the place to go to for answers to those kind of questions. In fact, nowhere in the Bible offers information like this. But we have been given a vision to live for, to work towards, to give us hope, purpose and joy. That's something to hold on to.

For reflection

How do we live all our relationships (with our human and non-human neighbours) now in light of what is to come? Take some time to think about the creatures with which you have meaningful interactions, because they share your local area, because they are one of your sources of food, because they are your pet or a way you make your income. How might you relate differently in the new creation? Is there anything you can do to align the two contexts more closely?

Prayer

Lord God, thank you for these beautiful verses and the future they show us. I can't wait for you to come and make things right, for your healing and restoration of this world. Help me bring you glory in how I live while things remain broken and hard. Amen.

Three-toothed orchid *Neotinea tridentata*

In 2022, A Rocha France launched an orchid protocol at the Domaine des Courmettes to see what they can learn about the health and evolution of the site's habitats from this excellent bio-indicator species.

Day 40

Joined in worship

Then I looked and heard the voice of many angels, numbering thousands upon thousands, and ten thousand times ten thousand. They encircled the throne and the living creatures and the elders. In a loud voice they were saying:

> **'Worthy is the Lamb, who was slain,**
> **to receive power and wealth and wisdom and strength and honour and glory and praise!'**

Then I heard every creature in heaven and on earth and under the earth and on the sea, and all that is in them, saying:

> **'To him who sits on the throne and to the Lamb**
> **be praise and honour and glory and power,**
> **forever and ever!'**

REVELATION 5:11–13

A while ago, one of my girls was blindsided by grief. It had been four years since she'd lost her grandmother, but there's nothing linear about loss and seemingly out of nowhere she was having a bad moment. 'I just want her to be here,' she wept. We were spending the day with a friend whose mother had died much more recently. This friend kindly jumped in to offer comfort: 'She is here! She's watching you *right now* from heaven.' Charis shot me a look. We debriefed later.

Over these 40 days, we've considered how the cross of Christ made healing, redemption and transformation possible across every relational axis: between humankind and God, between us as humans, between God and his creation, and between us humans and the rest of creation. In these verses from Revelation, we are given a glimpse of a future home where all of us will live together with joy and peace.

The subject of heaven is like a field beneath which an impossible number of bunnies have burrowed. You can barely put a foot down without risking a tumble down a deep and twisty hole. John's Patmos visions, captured as the book of Revelation, are responsible for more than their fair share of these holes. So many over the years have followed deep subterranean passages into dead ends of detail that this dreamy, inspiring apocalyptic literature was never intended to reveal. We might be tempted to stay away, fearful of the mysterious multi-eyed creatures, the cacophony of sound, the fearsome evil unleashing terror till its dying breath. But what beauty we'd miss if we did! What hope and sanity and glory John has bequeathed us.

Verse 11 gives the kind of cast list the average person on the street would say might be in heaven, should such a place exist, namely angels and people. Then comes verse 13. The original word translated here as 'heaven' (*ouranôi*) was the word for sky, firmament, the space above the earth, just as much as it was the word for where God dwells. With that in mind, every habitat is covered. Flying things, under- and on-the-ground things, watery things: every kind of creature brings its own praise to its maker. As the theologian Richard Bauckham puts it, 'The creation worships God just by being itself, as God made it, existing for God's glory.'[34] The biblical picture of our eternal future is incredibly biodiverse. The whole choir of creation will raise its voice in worship, and what a joyful noise we'll all make.

That may be an inspiring vision to keep us going on a grey day, but it is more than that. It dignifies those living things over which we have such power by placing us alongside each other as fellow worshippers. It reminds us we have something to learn, as those who struggle to give Jesus his due. God breathed his own life into us, made us image-bearers, gave us delegated responsibility to rule, so I'm not saying we don't have a special place in God's affections or purposes. The Bible is clear that we do. But these verses are another corrective to our tendency to abuse our position.

At the very centre of this scene depicted in Revelation is the Lamb – Jesus – not strung up for a humiliating execution but on a throne. Every other player on the stage is there to worship him: angels, elders, all the other living creatures. In the end, that's who we all are: worshippers. At peace with one another, we will be entirely free to be fully present and fully given to the purpose for which we were all made.

For reflection

Put yourself into this picture of the new heavens and new earth. What can you see? Hear? Smell? Touch? Where are you and what are you doing? What do you notice about Jesus?

Prayer

Lord God, there is so much that holds me back from worshipping you: distraction, doubt, self-consciousness, sin. Thank you that you have made creation to praise you by its very nature. I want to join in with the same wholehearted abandon. I can't wait for the day to come when we are all before your throne singing the same song. Until then, I will do my best and because of your grace and mercy and your sacrifice on the cross, that is enough. Amen.

Honey badger *Mellivora capensis*

The honey badger is one of the most elusive animals of the Indian jungle. In 2015, the team in India captured (by camera) the first documented occurrence in Bannerghatta National Park.

Six-week group discussion guide

Week one: The whole story

1 What have your experiences of Lent been like in the past?

2 What are your hopes (and/or fears) for this Lenten journey?

3 In the introduction to *The Whole Easter Story*, Jo writes:

> Often when considering the Easter story, we think in terms of what it means for our personal relationship with God. We are children of our times and places and – in wealthier societies anyway – we have a current obsession with the self. We are all about our own individual growth, purpose and spirituality.

Do you agree with this characterisation? Why or why not?

4 What is your current understanding of how the death and resurrection of Jesus offers redemption for us and for the rest of creation?

5 Read the whole of John 19 aloud twice. The first time, focus on engaging your imagination. What can you see, hear, smell and touch? Where are you in each scene and how do you feel as the shocking events unfold?

The second time, be attentive to any word or phrase that particularly stands out to you. What might God want to say to you?

Leave some time for silent reflection, and then share as you are willing.

Week two: God and people

1. Briefly share stories of how you came to have a relationship with God, and what that looks like in your life at the moment.

2. Read Romans 5:6–11. What do these verses say about humankind and the impact of Christ's death on our relationship with God? What changed because of the cross, and what stayed the same?

3. What does it mean for people to live as God's enemies?

4. How is life different for those who have accepted the gift of reconciliation?

5. 1 Corinthians 1:18 describes the cross as both foolishness and the very power of God. How do you see it? How do you feel about talking about the Easter story with family, friends or work colleagues who don't share your faith?

Week three: God and creation

1. Describe one of your favourite places in the great outdoors. What do you love about it? What memories do you have associated with it?

2. What does it mean in practice for God's kingdom to come on earth (Matthew 6:10)?

3. Romans 1:20 says: 'For since the creation of the world God's invisible qualities – his eternal power and divine nature – have been clearly seen, being understood from what has been made.' Which of God's qualities have you seen and understood from creation?

4. Read Colossians 1:15–20. Look at each occurrence of the phrase 'all things' (*ta panta*). What is the passage telling us about Christ and the whole creation?

5 How did creation respond to the birth, death and resurrection of Jesus? What should we notice and learn from these events?

Week four: Human relationships

1 Tell some stories (that are appropriate to share) from your own life or others about relationships God has redeemed and healed.

2 Jesus makes an inextricable link between his forgiveness of us and our forgiveness of others (Matthew 6:12). Why do you think this is?

3 In what ways does your church embody the love of God for every single person?

4 Read 1 John 4:16–21. What does God's love for us mean for how we relate to each other?

5 How do we move from hatred to love, especially when it comes to someone who has badly hurt us?

Week five: People and creation

1 In what ways are you in a relationship of interdependence with the rest of creation?

2 Read Genesis 2:15–20. What are the unique responsibilities we have in this world as God's image-bearers? What is the significance of the man's naming of the wild creatures?

3 What are the consequences when parts of God's creation are damaged by human activity or neglect?

4 Revelation 11:18 says God's judgement will come on those who destroy the earth. Who of us can say we haven't treated this world

badly to some degree? Of what do we need to repent in this regard, mindful that God's grace and mercy is – thankfully – boundless?

5 If Christ has redeemed all creation by his death, how should we live in that creation now?

Week six: Now and what is to come

1 Revisit the hopes you had for this Lent time together. Has it met your expectations? Any surprises or frustrations?

2 Has your understanding of the scope of God's redemptive purposes for the world changed through this time together? If so, how?

3 Read Matthew 28:1–10 twice over. As in our first week, when we read about the crucifixion, while reading the first time, focus on engaging your imagination. What can you see, hear, smell and touch? Where are you in each scene and how do you feel as events unfold?

The second time, be attentive to any word or phrase that particularly stands out to you. What might God want to say to you?

Leave some time for silent reflection, and then share as you are willing.

4 What are the implications for the here and now in the fact that the biblical picture of eternal life includes a restored and redeemed earth (see for example Romans 8:20–21 and Revelation 21:1)?

5 How do you most need the Holy Spirit's transforming power in your relationship with God, your fellow humans and with the wider creation?

Notes

1. John Stott, 'Foreword', in Peter Harris, *Under the Bright Wings* (Hodder and Stoughton, 1993), pp. ix–x.
2. You can hear more of Federica's story in the A Rocha *Field Notes* podcast, episode 38.
3. 'Evangelism and follow up: session 1', Life Bible-Presbyterian Church, **lifebpc.com/resources/evangelism-follow-up**
4. **urbandictionary.com/define.php?term=Love&page=3**
5. In *The Poems and Written Addresses of Mary T. Lathrap*, edited by Julia R. Parish (Women's Christian Temperance Movement of Michigan, 1895).
6. From Samuel Crossman's hymn 'My song is love unknown', 1664.
7. **talkingjesus.org/research/about-the-research**
8. **aa.org/the-twelve-steps**
9. For example, 1 Chronicles 21:1; Job 1:6; Luke 10:18.
10. See Revelation 21 as one place this is described.
11. John Stott, *The Message of Acts*, The Bible Speaks Today (IVP Academic, 2000).
12. 'Plastic pollution', *IUCN Issues Brief*, May 2024, **iucn.org/resources/issues-brief/plastic-pollution**
13. Bill McKibben, *The Comforting Whirlwind: God, Job and the scale of creation* (Cowley Publications, 2005), page number unavailable.
14. **gallup.com/cliftonstrengths/en/254033/strengthsfinder.aspx**
15. Eddie Izzard, *Glorious* (1997).
16. WWF, *Living Planet Report 2022: Building a nature-positive society*, October 2022, **wwf.org.uk/our-reports/living-planet-report-2022**
17. N.T. Wright, *Surprised by Hope: Rethinking heaven, the resurrection, and the mission of the church* (HarperOne, 2008), p. 104.
18. John 14:2–3, where Jesus talks about preparing a place for us to go, is sometimes used to argue that we 'go to heaven'. Wright, in *Surprised by Hope*, argues persuasively that the Greek refers to a temporary lodging, where believers who die go until they return with Christ to the renewed heavens and earth.
19. John Stott, '"In Christ": The meaning and implications of the gospel

of Jesus Christ', C.S. Lewis Institute, 3 June 2007, **cslewisinstitute.org/resources/in-christ-the-meaning-and-implications-of-the-gospel-of-jesus-christ**
20 Miranda Harris and Jo Swinney, *A Place at the Table: Faith, hope and hospitality* (Hodder and Stoughton, 2022), p. 143.
21 Department for Culture, Media and Sport, 'Gold framework – 2023 edition', **gov.uk/government/publications/gold-framework-2023-edition/gold-framework-2023-edition**
22 You can read about Charles Foster's adventures in depth in his book *Being a Beast* (Profile Books, 2016).
23 Simon Hattenstone, 'Going underground: meet the man who lived as an animal', *The Guardian*, 23 January 2016, **theguardian.com/environment/2016/jan/23/going-underground-meet-man-lived-as-animal-charles-foster**
24 **en.wikipedia.org/wiki/Hikikomori**
25 Dave Lawler, 'The global cities with the most and least green space', Axios, 3 May 2018, **axios.com/2018/05/03/the-cities-with-the-most-green-space-around-the-world**
26 **amnh.org/content/download/131241/2201972/file/human_microbiome_your_body_is_an_ecosystem_stepread1.pdf**
27 Lynn White Jr, 'The historical roots of our ecological crisis', *Science* 155, no. 3767 (1967), pp. 1203–07.
28 J.G. Speth, *Red Sky at Morning: America and the crisis of the global environment* (Yale University Press, 2005).
29 Released in 2022, written and directed by Ruben Östlund.
30 *The Matrix* was directed by Lana Wachowski and Lilly Wachowski, who were credited as the Wachowski Brothers at the time of the film's release in 1999.
31 The Netherlands: Sjerp de Vries, 'Local availability of green and blue space and prevalence of common mental disorders in the Netherlands', BJPsych Open 2:6 (2016), pp. 366–72, **ncbi.nlm.nih.gov/pmc/articles/PMC5609776**; Scotland: Jamie Hamilton, 'Outdoor learning: closing the attainment gap in primary schoolchildren in Scotland', Forestry Commission Scotland, February 2018, **cdn.forestresearch.gov.uk/2018/07/fcrn103.pdf**; Italy: Rita Berto, 'Exposure to restorative environments helps restore attentional capacity', *Journal of Environmental Psychology* 25 (2005), pp. 249–59, **greenplantsforgreenbuildings.org/wp-content/uploads/2020/02/Exposure_to_restorative_environments_hel.pdf**.
32 **blueletterbible.org/Comm/mhc/Deu/Deu_022.cfm**

33 Oliver M.T. O'Donovan, 'Where were you...?' in R.J. Berry (ed.), *The Care of Creation: Focusing concern and action* (IVP, 2000), p. 90.
34 Richard Bauckham, 'Stewardship and relationship', in Berry (ed.), *The Care of Creation*, p. 104.

Advent is a time to remember and reflect on the Christmas story and the baby at its heart. But the virgin birth, the manger, the mysterious eastern visitors and their portentous gifts – all these hint at a much grander narrative. Come and explore the whole Christmas story, and find your place within it.

The Whole Christmas Story
An Advent adventure through Genesis, Revelation and points in between
Jo Swinney
978 0 85746 941 0 £8.99

brfonline.org.uk

Lent is traditionally a time of repentance, fasting and prayer as we prepare to celebrate our salvation at Easter. Through daily readings and reflections from Ash Wednesday to Easter Day, Amy Scott Robinson explores different biblical images of repentance, sin, forgiveness and grace, bringing them together in Holy Week as a lens through which to view Christ's work of reconciliation on the cross.

Images of Grace
A journey from darkness to light at Easter
Amy Scott Robinson
978 1 80039 117 8 £9.99

brfonline.org.uk

BRF Ministries

Inspiring people of all ages to grow in Christian faith

BRF Ministries is the home of Anna Chaplaincy, Living Faith, Messy Church and Parenting for Faith

As a charity, our work would not be possible without fundraising and gifts in wills.
To find out more and to donate, visit brf.org.uk/give or call +44 (0)1235 462305

Registered with FUNDRAISING REGULATOR